The Uh-oh Squad

A TALE OF SUBSTANCE ABUSE

The Uh-oh Squad

BY DENI GORDON

With Illustrations by Rainbow Astin

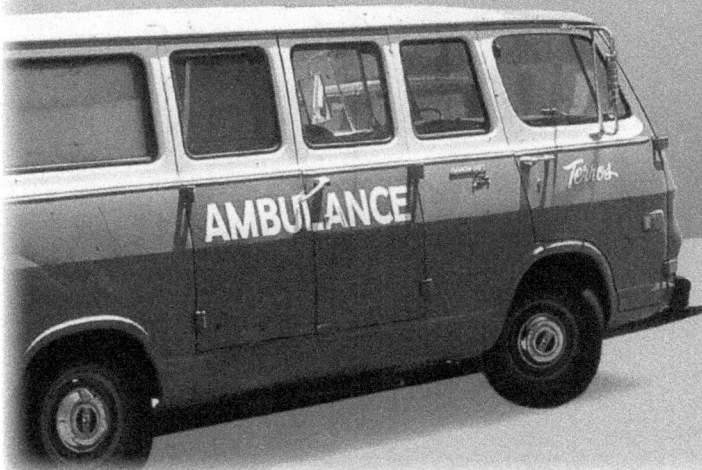

GusGus Press • Bedazzled Ink Publishing
Fairfield, California

978-1-949290-17-2 paperback

Cover Design
by
Meg Larkin

Photographs were provided by Joseph Meserve,
"a friend who shared the many of the adventures with me."

GusGus Press
a division of
Bedazzled Ink Publishing Company
Fairfield, California
http://www.bedazzledink.com

*Dedicated to my family and all the people
with whom I've shared the shotgun seat.*

Prologue

Leaving was the hardest thing I ever did. It wasn't just a job and co-workers that I left; it was my home and family. Like any family, we had our share of ups and downs in those six years.

This is the true story of six years of working in a Phoenix drug abuse agency. As they say on TV, "the names have been changed to protect the innocent."

I began as a volunteer in the clinic and ended as a supervisor (Head staff) in crisis, Director of Training and Research Coordinator. Well, even in families, people have many different roles.

Photographs were provided by Joseph Meserve, a friend who shared the many adventures with me.

Chapter 1

The Beginning of Everything

TERROS was about three years old when I began volunteering in 1972. It was started by a young man named Jack and some of his friends. All of the "founding fathers" were seventeen years old. Their goal was to take care of another friend who was "bumming out" on STP. STP can be either an amphetamine-based hallucinogen or a motor oil; however, in this case, it was the hallucinogen. The friends shuffled the "bummer" around for a week to different homes until he was normal again. There were few people or agencies willing to take care of "dopers." Many didn't want to admit to the existence of drug abuse problems and many others had no idea how to treat them. Victims were left to die or to be accidentally discovered in garbage cans. The lucky ones were left on the lawn or parking lots of the local hospitals. There was fear surrounding associating with drug abusers and there were no facilities to treat users or addicts.

After the incident with their friend, Jack and his friends spent months talking with teachers, doctors, city council members, and anyone willing to listen about the lack of help available to dopers and people suffering chronic or acute mental illness. Discussions led to the development of a place for crisis intervention and non-punitive medical and psychological treatment. Initially, money was obtained by car washes, bake sales, raffles, and donations from organizations such as the Elks. A few physicians and psychologists began volunteering their assistance and eventually approached the County Medical Society. This led to a coordinating agency to coordinate fund-raising, and speaking with various public and private agencies to enlist the services of doctors.

They applied for federal funds available to create drug abuse programs, and especially to establish a Detox (detoxification) center. We even joined the telethon fund-raising circuit! In 1969, Jack and his friends incorporated, but the agency name was misspelled on the papers: Terra became TERROS. We spent a lot of time explaining that the only significance of our name was an error in touch-typing. We rented an old two-story house in a run-down area of Phoenix. Neighbors complained to the city about a drug abuse agency moving in, attracting "those sorts of people."

When the medical Clinic opened in 1970, they were less hostile and began to take advantage of the services in the free clinic. The police agreed to "no heat," (nonintervention), but only as long as no illegal drugs were on the property. We received donations of medical equipment, supplies, and medications from some of the local physicians and hospitals. Some of the supplies included items we could never use and some of the medications were not appropriate for our clientele.

In the beginning, we purchased a dozen pagers and a telephone system with four lines. Staff received a "salary" of twenty-five dollars per month and was constantly on-call. Everyone had to carry a pager with them all the time. Early on, grant money was limited, so staff would use their private vehicles to go to the client. After evaluating the problem, staff would either remain with the client at the home or provide transport to the nearest hospital. We would find a phone (there were no cell phones at that time) to call base and let them know what was happening. Sometimes we had to stop at a gas station en route to a hospital with a client to notify the hospital that we were coming or to tell base what was going on.

Tori was one of the original Crisis staff. She drove a motor scooter, the type a slow runner could pass. I had to chuckle when I imagine her carting an overdose to the hospital on the back of her "putt-putt." Tori and I frequently treated six-foot tall, two-hundred-fifty pounders. I used to imagine her putting-putting along with a six-foot, semi-conscious male barely able to hang on to Tori or the bike. What she did was to actually call base and request someone with a car to meet her to transport the client. Sometimes base had to call several off-duty staff to find someone with a car available to meet Tori and carry the client to the hospital. Eventually she bought a red Volvo with big tail fins and earned the nickname "Batwoman."

Local funds gradually increased and larger grants were obtained from the federal government. Although we were being accepted as a valuable substance abuse treatment center by the "ESTABLISHMENT," many street people and dopers did not yet trust TERROS. We would get a call about an overdose from a "friend." The overdose was left in an empty house or an alley for us to discover. Frequently, the overdose was dumped into a trash can to "save them from the police." When we went out on a call we were rarely looking for a structure, instead we would look for garbage cans or large cardboard boxes. Sometimes the helping friend would bring their overdosed friend to TERROS, drive in front of the house, kick the body onto the lawn, and then drive away. Occasionally, they would honk to make sure their friend was found.

By 1972, the house included Crisis, outpatient Detox for opiates, long-term Counseling, and a Clinic to treat venereal disease and general medical problems. Inpatient Detox was at the county hospital about a mile from the house. Crisis had a five-year-old dark green-and-white van "ambulance" with a flat, lumpy mattress on the floor in the back. All staff learned basic counseling techniques from members of the Counseling Department and emergency first aid and medications from physicians.

Crisis staff worked a twenty-four hour on-duty shift, and a forty-eight hour on-call shift per week. Members of the other departments, including the directors, had to work one twelve hour Crisis shift per week. As time went on and our training and equipment improved, staff no longer had to either stay at the client's house or take the client to the hospital. All of the training now allowed us to bring the client to TERROS to be treated or monitored. Some of the clients were too critical to be monitored by us and we would transport them to the nearest hospital. This is where I came in.

I had just begun to work part-time on my Master of Science degree and full time at a hospital lab. My dream of attending medical school was fading, since great numbers of women were not being admitted in those days. Admission committees asked many questions about my view of premarital sex, Vietnam, and whether I would quit when I got pregnant. I felt I was interviewing for a political position. They weren't interested in my medical aspirations, only in whether my sex life would interfere, and cause me to waste a seat a "deserving" male could use. I have no idea what kinds of questions male applicants faced, but pregnancy and premarital sex were probably not among them.

My family didn't understand my medical aspirations and had a hard time being supportive. My parents would say, "Become a nurse and marry a doctor. Women don't become doctors." I felt alone and like a failure. My already slight self-confidence was quickly fading with my dreams. I wanted to do something to get out of my rut of depression, and to be with people who were not judgmental. I watched the TERROS telethon and thought it would be fun to work with them. I called and offered to volunteer in the TERROS Clinic a couple of nights per week. My family had always labeled me the "rebel," and I had spent most of my life "on the outside." My social life had been limited to only rarely seeing people outside of work. I felt that the people at TERROS were interested in whom, not what, a person was. I never would have predicted that in the process my social skills would improve, and I would become more self-confident and self-respecting.

As I drove into the gravel driveway of the TERROS house, I wondered what I was getting into. Most of the buildings in the neighborhood should have been condemned twenty years earlier. TERROS looked no better, although it had an old coat of no longer bright yellow paint and a small lawn with green grass. I climbed four cracked cement steps to the porch. The front door was a funny color of green and displayed two signs: a left arrow for Crisis, Clinic, and Business and a right arrow for Detox. As I looked to the right, I saw a partially covered driveway where a green-and-white van was parked. In time, I discovered that this house was originally the home of some very wealthy folks when Phoenix was a young town, some seventy-five years earlier. The building had undergone many transitions, including serving as a boarding house and possibly even a brothel, before becoming TERROS. I wandered around to take a look at the place. In the back was a small two-story building, used by us as a storage shed, which once had been the servants' quarters. Between the shed and the house, pavement replaced the gravel and I was to find out later that rumors were that the paved area once had been a tennis court.

Deni Gordon

I entered through the front door on the left because I was going to volunteer in the Clinic. There was a room with three folding chairs, two wooden chairs, a large armchair, and a telephone on a card table directly ahead of me. To the right, I saw a long hallway. There were three rooms on the west side, with windows overlooking the gravel parking lot, and two rooms on the east side. A bathroom was at the end of the hall.

I was greeted by a staff member wearing cut-off Levi's and an old blue shirt, who introduced himself as Jared. He was about five foot eight, with dark hair to his shoulders and a broad grin. He seemed to bounce like Tigger from *Winnie the Pooh* as he directed me to the Clinic. I made a sharp right, past the fireplace, and crossed a very large living room with a coat of fading blue paint. In the living room was a standard office-size metal desk directly under the front window, a couch, two recliners, and some beanbag chairs. There was a nine-inch black-and-white TV atop a broken console television. I was told that the console TV had not worked in at least eight years and was being used as a desk. Someone was at the metal desk, staring outside, listening for the tell-tale sounds of a body being dumped on the lawn or in the driveway.

The living room

The living room

About halfway through the living room was a wide wooden staircase with the same black-grey carpet. I continued to walk through the living room, past the stairway and to the left was another room. This room served as the waiting room for the Clinic. There was a door by the driveway. There was another room that served as the office to the Clinic. The green-and-white van in the driveway could be seen through the window.

The Clinic office was a small room with a desk and two large metal cabinets that opened to an exam room on either side. If two people walked into the Clinic at the same time, they had to hold their breath to pass each other back to back. The exam rooms were smaller than an average doctor's exam room. Each held a donated gynecologic exam table, cabinets with dressings and equipment, such as a blood pressure cuff. The black-grey carpet extended into the Clinic office.

At the end of my first week in the Clinic, I was sitting in the living room with Jared, and he filled in some of the history of TERROS for me. All of the furniture had been donated. We were sure that the local dump refused to accept the pieces and we worried about where we could eventually be able to dispose of the furniture. There were no hazardous materials dump sites at that time, but if there were, I think they would not have taken the furniture either. I think we were an acceptable place to not only dump bodies but also furniture and supplies. The furniture, like the medical supplies and medications, were given to us because no one knew what else to do with them. Some of the stuff was useful and some was not.

The couch was a dark color that was no longer identifiable. Its cushions had the permanent shape of someone sitting on them. Whatever springs had been present had sprung long ago. I had the feeling that a crane would be required to lift anyone sitting to a standing position from that couch, especially if they weighed over seventy-five pounds. The recliners were large and brown with visible springs sticking out. The number of beans in the beanbag chairs could have been easily counted on one hand. According to Jared, the furniture was being held together by the crabs (scabies) holding hands with the lice. The most comfortable place to sit was on the floor, although you never really knew what was living in the carpet. The whole house was covered with a dirty black-grey shag carpet, although I suspected it was originally a lighter color. The shag was probably originally long, but you couldn't prove it by looking. There were probably lice and crabs living in the carpet on food that had been dropped on the floor, along with the mud and dirt from hundreds of trampling feet.

We replaced some of the furniture two years later. Now our couch was brown and white and had comfortable cushions. The old furniture was left at the dump and we drove away very rapidly before they could stop us and make us take it back. Even in this neighborhood there was no one desperate enough to take it!

The new couch

Mitch was the Clinic Director. He was a twenty-five-year-old, blonde-haired RN I introduced myself and explained about my medical background and hospital training. I explained that I had worked in hospitals since I was sixteen. I told him that I had been trying to go medical school, but was turned down because I was a woman trying to enter a "male" career.

Mitch seemed overjoyed with a new volunteer already trained in medical exams and treatment. He informed me that our responsibility would be to provide an initial assessment and triage. The doctor would then see those people needing medications. Mitch explained that we had a grant from County Health to do V.D. (STD) testing and screening from five to six p.m. We would screen and test clients in the clinic. Anyone suspected to be positive for V.D. was to remain until the doctor arrived. They would then receive either penicillin or tetracycline and a report made to the health department.

General Clinic hours began at six p.m., or whenever the doctor arrived. There were about eight local physicians who volunteered their time regularly and nine others would help out occasionally. The Medical Director of Detox would bail us out if the scheduled doctor couldn't come. Mitch said that we could see any problem during general Clinic. We treated urinary tract infections, pregnancy, colds, sniffles, diarrhea, headaches, and almost every other type of problem. The county hospital appreciated that we relieved their emergency room of some non-emergency traffic, so they would sterilize our equipment as gratitude.

The metal cabinets in the office held donated medications: cough and cold preps, antibiotics, birth control pills, and a few miscellanies that we would never use. Some of the donated medications were out of date, a few expired three years earlier, and we had to check this carefully. Once a week, we would clean out the cabinet and toss out expired meds. Mitch explained the system of record keeping used for Clinic and how it differed from Crisis paper work.

During my orientation, people began filling up the Clinic waiting room. It held two more very old couches with mean springs ready to attack unsuspecting buttocks, a beanbag without many beans, a beanbag chair with no beans, and the same black-grey carpet. There was literature about V.D., hepatitis, and birth control on the bookshelves and end tables. Some of the pamphlets were in English, some in Spanish.

Mitch called in the first client and showed me how to fill out the paperwork. He took the exam room on the south side and I took the north one. Things moved so fast that I didn't have time for an anxiety attack. I didn't even notice that we had to inhale and turn sideways to pass each other. We saw twenty people for V.D. checks that hour. The six or so possible positives were asked to stay for the doc. The doc arrived at 6:20 p.m. and we began shaking the penicillin, preparing to treat them.

Penicillin is a very thick suspension, similar to natural creamy peanut butter, and the oil layer separates from the penicillin easily. If the vial is not shaken well each time it is used, the oil liquid is removed and remaining penicillin begins to resemble cement in its consistency. One night I was filling a syringe with penicillin, but I was too busy to notice that much of the oil had been removed. I didn't even realize that I had to pull very hard to draw the penicillin into the syringe. The suction on the syringe was so intense that the needle blew off as I was preparing to inject the client, hitting the ceiling, and covering the walls and me with penicillin. After the initial shock of the needle flying off and being bathed in penicillin, Mitch and I just doubled over in laughter. Even the client started laughing. The doctor didn't think it was so funny ... what a stuffed shirt!

The V.D. Clinic was an interesting experience. It was amazing how many people claimed to have caught the disease from doorknobs. I almost began to believe it, especially after a large group of people arrived in the Clinic from Jerome, a ghost town in northern Arizona. Every one of them claimed that they had not had sexual contact with anyone. They all explained that the doorknobs in town were pretty old and probably contaminated. One woman exposed to V.D. was awaiting the dreaded injections. I shook the vial and drew the penicillin into two syringes and entered the exam room. She had dropped her pants, exposing a very large, colorful tattoo of a butterfly covering both buttocks. I had to give the injections into the wing tips. I felt like an animal abuser and expected to be picked up by the SPCA.

The general Clinic would begin approximately after the V.D. clinic. Women requesting birth control pills were examined by the doctor and tested for V.D. Shooters, intravenous drug users, with abscesses received antibiotics for the infections they got from using dirty needles, and the abscesses were opened. Babies and adults with coughs and sniffles received antihistamines or antibiotics appropriate for the age and cause of the problem.

During Clinic hours, the green van left and returned several times with overdoses or adverse drug reactions. Mitch, the doc, or I would then go into Crisis to evaluate the client's problem. By 10:00 p.m., we had treated about forty-five people for a wide range of problems. We helped the doctor finish all of the paperwork. As we collapsed on one of the ancient dilapidated couches, Mitch asked if I could return the next night. I worked every night that first week, and it went the same way each night. The second week, I came in on Wednesday. That was when I discovered that Mitch didn't always communicate well. He forgot to tell me that I was now a part-time staff member, was expected every week night and would receive twenty-five dollars per month. His face became flaming red as he screamed that I had missed the required staff meeting. I just stood there with my mouth wide open as if I was biting into an elephant. I was unaccustomed to being screeched at; plus I already had a job that would actually pay my rent. When he calmed down and his face regained its normal color, we reached a compromise. I would work three days in Clinic and the required Crisis shift, but was able to miss staff meetings if I was at my "real" job.

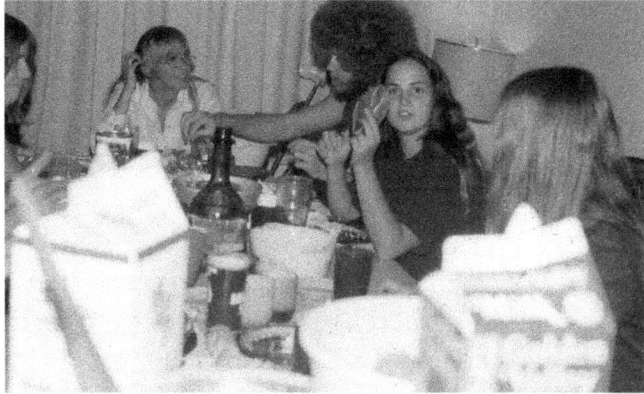

Administrators' meeting

Crisis was in charge of the twenty-four-hour hotline, the green-and-white van "ambulance," and handled the bodies dumped on the lawn. Clients walking in from the street were greeted by someone from Crisis. Sometimes, the individual needed just to talk or be evaluated for a drug reaction. They handled crisis counseling as well as the drug medical problems. Jared was an excellent representative of Crisis, ready to pounce at any time.

The third week, I showed up for my first staff meeting. We learned that we had received approval for ambulance status from the Corporation Commission. One of the local service clubs had donated money for us to buy a real ambulance to replace our green van, complete with sirens, lights, and radios. All staff members, including the Director, Controller, and secretary were required to attend Phoenix College and obtain training as an Emergency Medical Technician (EMT). EMT training was a new requirement for all ambulance personnel.

We had to enroll quickly because all ambulances in the county were sending their personnel and the class was filling up. In addition, all non-crisis staff were now required to work a twelve-hour Crisis shift. The Crisis staff continued to work four twelve-hour or two twenty-four hour shifts, be on-call, and attend staff meetings. Each Crisis shift consisted of three staff members, two would go out in the ambulance and one stayed at base. There were often one or more volunteers and a few off duty staff who came by to visit. The one who remained was responsible for the phones, walk-ins, overdoses dumped on the lawn, contact with the ambulance, and notifying the hospital if the ambulance was en route there. We could rotate who did what job. There was an effort to schedule people so that at least one fresh individual would begin a shift every twelve hours.

I had a feeling that my other job was about to be replaced. I met all the staff members at that meeting. The staff consisted of fifteen people in Levis, shorts, bathing trunks, sandals, hiking boots, or bare feet. Some of the men had beards and long hair, hanging past their shoulder blades. Everyone greeted me as though we had been friends for at least nine years. Most of the staff members were in their early or middle twenties.

Tom was Director of the agency; Steve headed Crisis; David ran Counseling. Mr. Clean, Director of Detox, had a shaved head and a gold front tooth with a diamond. He was a large man with a rather ominous appearance. Jack, the founder of TERROS, was a Crisis staff member and consulted Tom on how the agency should run. It seemed the only ones with professional training were two RNs, Mitch and Margaret, and the three counselors, all MSWs (Master of Social Work). I decided I was going to like working in a non-judgmental, relaxed environment, and I delighted with not having to wear uniforms. I was concerned about how to pay my rent and bills however.

Staff discussion

It was also announced that the Board of Directors decided to rent a second house in Tempe near the university. Once we had our real ambulance, the green van would become Unit Two. We raised enough money to equip it with a radio, sirens, and lights to service Tempe and Mesa areas. There were far fewer calls coming into the Tempe house than the Phoenix house. The house in Tempe eventually became a place for R and R, to relax after craziness in the Phoenix house. I think that was the only one of the non-boring staff meetings I attended in six years.

I found myself spending every free minute I had at TERROS. I joined the ranks of off duty staff that spent most of their time hanging around the house. There was no such thing as a routine day. Even the craziness of the Clinic seemed tame compared to Crisis. For the first time in my adult life I was accepted as a competent person, instead of being looked upon as a strange woman wanting to do man's work.

School was not a topic of discussion at TERROS. It was many years before I discovered that many of the staff were attending either college or graduate school. People who needed time to study or write a paper would elect to stay at base when there was a call and pretend to write letters to their family. Sometimes, the students would trade shifts and stay "home" to study. There was an unspoken ethic; no one asked about background history or future aspirations of staff. As the closet college kids eventually came out of the closet, most stated that school was not mentioned for fear of ridicule. Vietnam vets wanted to forget their tour and the public contempt. Many of the staff had at least experimented with drugs.

After three months of working at the Clinic, I got the chance to work my first Crisis shift with Tim and Sam. It was a quiet winter night at the Phoenix house with few phone calls and no walk-ins. It was so slow that we didn't even have off-duty staff visiting or volunteers— so I went upstairs to explore. Tim and Sam had a raging fire going in the fireplace downstairs and they sat in front of it discussing the different types of airplanes used by the Air Force. I think one or both had been in the military because military equipment was a frequent topic of conversation when they were together.

Upstairs were offices for Tom, the secretary, the comptroller (nicknamed "Hot Lips"), and the three counselors. I had discovered a small storeroom filled with boxes of medications donated over the years. No one seemed to know what was in those boxes. During this quiet shift, I decided to investigate the mysterious boxes to see if there was anything of use.

I discovered that some of the drugs had expired five years earlier and some would never be used by an agency such as ours. I took on the tedious task of stocking the Clinic with the useful medications and flushing the outdated pills. David, our resident crisis staff cartoonist later drew a picture showing the sewer rats getting loaded from our discarded drugs and staggering around the sewers. I decided that the injectable medications and other liquids were to be placed into boxes for transport to the dump and smashed by a tractor. It would have taken a year or more to open the ampoules and pour the contents into the toilet. The tractor was a more practical solution. I had been upstairs about two hours sorting through the boxes and finally decided it was time to stop for a while.

I walked to the top of the staircase and asked Sam to help me bring the boxes I had sorted and packed downstairs. I explained that we needed to set them aside to be taken to the dump. Sam came upstairs but continued the conversation with Tim. He was not listening to me when I explained what was in the boxes and what the plan was for their disposal. Sam carried the containers downstairs and instead of piling them in a corner to be taken to the dump the next day, he casually tossed the contents into the fireplace.

At that point, Sam's conversation with Tim was now focused on the types of bombs carried by different military planes. I started to try to say something but then realized that it was too late and I knew I would not be able to interrupt them. I decided to patiently wait for the punctuation to their conversation so I sat on the fourth step from the bottom of the staircase, a safe distance away from the fireplace. As the vials heated and expanded, there was a hissing sound and then the tops blew off. The superheated liquids shot out of the fireplace with beautiful colored flames. Sam and Tim dove behind couches while continuing their discussion. As the "bombs burst in midair," conversationally and literally, one of our regular alcoholic clients walked in, paused, and then began marching and singing some strange mashup of the *Battle Hymn of the Republic*, *America* and the theme from *M*A*S*H*. I began laughing so hard that I rolled down the stairs.

The next Crisis shift I worked with Sam and Tim was also relatively quiet. Six people crowded together on the lumpy couch and the floor to watch *M*A*S*H* on the nine-inch TV. *M*A*S*H* became our theme show and we always hoped that there were no calls during the show. If anyone had a client during the show, someone was assigned to take notes on the show. An acid bummer (bad acid trip) and a speed overamp (too much speed), were the only clients of the evening. They had been treated and sent merrily on their way earlier in the shift. Later, after visiting staff had departed, Sam fell asleep on a Clinic couch and Tim dozed in the recliner, I began to snooze also. Suddenly, at about five a.m., the morning paperboy pitched the paper with an extra effort and it banged against the front door. Tim and Sam jumped up. Tim grabbed a broom and charged out, Sam ran out behind him. They raced around the building shouting, "Who's there?" They never explained what the purpose of the broom was, but their faces were bright red upon their return. They did, however, bring in the paper.

One of the constant duties of both Clinic and Crisis Staff was to record daily shift reports in the communication log (com log) detailing phone calls, walk-ins, and calls. Jared, a Crisis staff member, recorded his daily shift reports in the com log in what we called "Star Trekisms." One of the better and more confusing entries read:

STARDATE 11, 2035. TODAY WE SAW AND WERE EATEN BY A GREEN ALIEN IN GYM

He also named our administrative staff after characters in *M*A*S*H*, based on their corresponding personalities. Tom became Colonel Blake, Steve was Frank Burns, and Carla, the comptroller, resembled Major "Hot Lips" Hoolihan. Shifts with Jared were usually an unpredictable, but interesting experience, similar to his entries in the com log.

One night, Jared told Tim and me a story about a ghost who lived upstairs in the Phoenix house. He swore that he had seen the ghost in a long white wedding gown. Tim and I were rather doubtful; after all, Jared did have an active imagination and no one else had ever seen this supposed resident ghost. I never saw it when I was cleaning out the medication closet at night. A few weeks later when Jared, Tim, and I worked together again, Jared got involved with a suicide rap (talking to an individual who was contemplating suicide), Tim and I took our life-size training mannequin, wrapped it in a white sheet (we didn't have a wedding gown handy), and stood it behind an upstairs door. Several hours later, Jared went upstairs and discovered the "ghost."

When he returned, he was pale, hyperventilating, and ready to collapse. Tim and I were astonished when we learned of his discovery but we couldn't remain astonished long and started laughing. Jared started pouting about our "nasty" trick and would not talk to us. Jared was still pouting hours later when the shift was almost over but recovered his sense of humor when we drove the green van to meet the police across town.

Police had stopped a man who was wandering down the middle of a busy main street and who was not aware of his surroundings. The police wanted us to evaluate him and take him to where he would not be in danger. Our crazy friend was loudly expounding about ghosts coming from televisions produced in Boise. He wanted to warn civilization to protect themselves from Boise televisions! Our evaluation and his on-going narrative led us to the conclusion that he had quit taking his Thorazine (medication to alleviate hallucinations).

After we left the client at the county psychiatric facility, I told Jared that we obviously had a TV made in Boise and we were too late for redemption from ghosts. All three of us eventually forgot about the "ghost" upstairs. Residents of the upstairs offices were less than excited with their pre-caffeine discovery that morning. We tried to perfect the innocent "who me?" look as the building rocked from them yelling at us. Our "ghost" was not mentioned in the com log, although the "Boise TV ghosts" were.

The Medical Director offered to teach several of us from the Clinic and Crisis how to suture. He showed us how to suture hotdogs. We brought in about ten packages of hot dogs to practice suturing every chance we got. We had about six "patients" left the day the doctor was going to evaluate our suture technique. Unfortunately, that day one of the staff cooked and ate our "patients" for lunch before the doc could examine our work. Suddenly the house became filled with suture students screaming at the "evil wiener eater." There were threats of violence and how the evil wiener eater was going to need sutures. The offender screamed that he had been too busy on his shift to eat. To keep peace, the doc brought in a package of hot dogs so we could take the final exam. There was a lot of grumbling about the "sanctity of the refrigerator," but we were all friends again.

I had a chance to use my new suture training a few nights later. A young man named Bryan arrived in the clinic bleeding from a long laceration on his arm. He wore a bicycle chain around his waist, and was accompanied by his "bodyguard." Bryan and I would meet many times for the same problem. He stood about five foot three inches and had a "short man complex." He said the bicycle chain was to protect him, but I explained that it invited other people to challenge him to fights. I'm not sure what the other guy looked like, but Bryan always needed to be sutured. Mitch or I sewed him up, unless the wound was too deep and then the surgeon at Maricopa County Hospital had to repair the injuries. Bryan and I talked frequently about the bicycle chain and how it was an invitation to be attacked. This went on for two years.

There was a point where I hadn't seen him for six months and hoped he hadn't died from one of his fights. One night soon after that Bryan showed up at TERROS, handed me the bicycle chain, and walked out without saying a word. About a year and a half later he returned to introduce me to his wife and tell me about the college program he was attending. Suddenly, I knew all the time and talk was worthwhile.

The day our "real" ambulance arrived there was a great deal of excitement. It was a white Dodge van with a blue stripe and the TERROS logo. It had a light bar on top with red and blue emergency lights, "gumballs" in ambulance jargon. The interior was marbled blue and white with blue Plexiglas doors covering the cabinets. We had a real gurney instead of a lumpy old mattress.

New ambulance

We felt like we had hit the big time. We bought a new fishing tackle box and stocked it with dressings, blood pressure cuffs, stethoscopes, and medications, ipecac to induce vomiting, aspirin, cherry syrup vitamin B 12 placebos, etc. We named the box Alice's Restaurant, after the Arlo Guthrie song popular at that time. We stocked the cabinets with restraints, extra dressings, blankets for infants, airways, oxygen masks and tubing, IV tubing and IV saline and glucose.

One of the Detox staff, Big Jim, wanted to buy the old green van for his personal use. He was referred for psychiatric help. The decision to retire the green van was arrived at when it died in the middle of a busy intersection during code three traffic with an observer from the State Department of Health and Emergency Services.

At the staff meeting that week, Steve showed us how to use the ambulance lights and sirens and how to make FCC approved radio transmissions. We learned our code letters, standard emergency codes, and how to use the new radio installed in the house for dispatching. We no longer had to search out pay phones or keep change in our pockets!

The upgrade in our vehicles was accompanied by a change in radio frequency. We were trying out different antennae locations which required different frequencies and new call letters. In the course of two months we had to learn seven new sets of call letters. We tried to have the current call letters written on a piece of paper attached to the dashboard, but with all the changes, scratching out the old and writing the new letters, we considered ourselves lucky to be able to communicate with anyone this side of Mars. One day during this period, Hot Lips sat in the middle of an intersection with the lights and siren on, trying to find the most current call letters so she could report our patient's change in status. I was in the back, embarrassed and glad that no one could see into the van.

One of the frequencies we used was shared by some group of farmers. Early morning transmissions consisted of the grain report and number of new animals munching in the field. It became frustrating trying to radio the Base when the farmers were discussing the cattle. One day I had to radio information for the hospital, but was unable to get through. The farmers were clogging the frequency with a debate about whether to call the vet because the placenta was stuck. I cannot repeat my thoughts on the topic. We eventually got a new frequency that was not shared with the farmers.

Our new ambulance acquired its first dent the second day of its life in the field. We were en route code three to a possible overdose. Some drunk decided to race us, lost control, and spun into the ambulance. We had to radio for assistance on the original call, us *and* the drunk. But, at least we didn't have to find a payphone!

After that, Steve and Tom then threatened us with a fate worse than death if anything were to happen to the ambulance. David, the staff artist, drew a series of cartoons depicting Steve and Tom guarding the ambulance with machine guns and a tank.

The threats were useless however, because within a week, Crisis staffers, Mark and Linda, sheared the gumballs going through an apartment overhang. The "hot dog war" was relegated to a mild disagreement in comparison to the "gumball war." David drew cartoons showing two tarred and feathered staff members wired atop the van, holding flashlights and spinning around. Unsurprisingly, about six months later, these same two unfortunate staff members sheared the gumballs off at the drive thru bank while cashing their paychecks.

I had been working in the Clinic six months and was making a hundred dollars per month. I decided to resign my other job, although I wasn't sure how 1 would meet my bills. Mitch and I got into an argument, his red face and screeching setting off my temper. I simply could not tolerate being screamed at. I resigned the Clinic that night and immediately began working fulltime in Crisis. At least the increased hours would ensure I'd make enough to pay my rent and other bills.

TERROS may have gained an international reputation for its success with drug abusers, but not international repute for salary. We still raised money with telethons, bake sales, and donations from a variety of community organizations. We even talked to many businesses about donations and explained how our presence could help cut down theft in their businesses.

Chapter 2

Crisis To Go

Stimulant Drugs, Uppers or Speed

I was scheduled for my first twenty-four hour shift the same day we had one of our usual boring staff meetings. The board members from the community and staff were sitting on the floor of the living room while the board members were telling us that central heat was going to be installed during the week. It was a hundred and ten degrees outside and probably one hundred twenty-five degrees in the house. This announcement was met with a minimum of calm logic and an abundance of sweat and shouting. We wanted air conditioning, or at least a fan; Mother Nature provided enough heat! After all, we were in Phoenix, Arizona, a desert town! In the middle of the shouting match, a very small woman who stood about four feet six inches and about as big around as a toothpick, weighing probably no more than sixty pounds, bounced into the house stark naked, waving a fluffy pink feather. Her name was Ginger, and she looked like a woman in her sixties. We later learned she was actually in her late teens.

The only clothing item Ginger wore were pink socks on her feet (I guess the sidewalk was really hot, after all it *was* a hundred and ten degrees that day). She danced and hopped over all the people on the floor, then danced out without saying a word.

This brought the staff meeting to a standstill. We sat with our mouths gaping! Everyone was trying to deny what they had just seen. Perhaps this was just a mass hallucination from the heat? I wondered if she had not just completed a twenty-four shift and this was an indication of what I had to look forward to.

There was total silence in the room until Jared stood up and yelled, "Reality Check!" Everyone began muttering under their breath.

Within ten minutes, we heard an incredible scream from outside. We ran out to find that this Ginger had pulled the stop sign out of the ground, cement block still attached, and was swinging the pole over her head, while screaming at green demons. No one was sure how to deal with her. The risk of decapitation was too great to approach her with the stop sign swinging around. A cop driving by radioed for help, jumped from his unit, and hid behind my five-foot, three-inch body. Other officers arrived and formed a line behind him. I felt like the leader of a parade without the drum major's baton. The entry in the com log was:

STARDATE 19,2135: A RED OCTAGON ATTACKED A NAKED LADY. SHE SUCCESSFULLY FOUGHT IT OFF!

David finished his counseling session and came outside to see what the excitement was all about. As crazy as things could get around TERROS, it wasn't every day that a short naked woman stood in the yard swinging a stop sign, screaming, observed by a parade of police hiding behind a slightly taller clothed woman (me). David then used his best counseling voice to "get into" her delusion, loudly counting the number of dead demons and eventually telling her that she got them all and we were all safe. Ginger finally agreed to put down the sign and we transported her to County Psych.

This poor young woman was the first person I had met who "burned her brain" with chronic speed use. She will never be a thinking person again, nor will she be likely to leave the state mental hospital. The last time I had checked on her, she was on antipsychotic medication and was suffering from side effects of the medication called dystonia and dyskinesia. She would walk around the hospital grounds with her head pulled to her shoulder, her hands making a pill-rolling motion and moving her mouth involuntarily.

The city replaced the stop sign with a traffic light. I wondered if they were trying to challenge the next speed freak that needed to defend themselves from aliens from space.

A common saying among people working in a crisis environment is: IF A CRISIS DOES NOT EXIST, CREATE ONE! We had been relatively slow for a week but life was not dull. Installation of the heating unit had begun but the temperature outside was one hundred and five degrees and above, while it was usually well over a hundred and nine degrees inside. Someone decided to build a wall separating the living room crisis department from outpatient detox. Our skills as counselors and medics far exceeded our skills as carpenters so the extra-large doorway had a funny slant at the top. We could never find a door to fit correctly. I never could understand the reason for the wall or the extra-large doorway.

The comptroller was infuriated at Mr. Clean because he hadn't cashed his paychecks for six months. The record keeper was yelling at me about my entry in an ambulance log. As I said earlier, I hate being yelled at so I had a bit of a temper tantrum and ripped the log into tiny little pieces after the second time he waved it in front of my nose. Steve made me tape the log back together.

Female staff was fighting with male staff because one couple had broken up. During this week of arguing, other couples began to break up and take sides. The staff cartoon showed the female "armed camp" facing the male "armed camp" separated by a boundary sign reading "No Man's Land." Bras and jock straps were depicted as camouflage for artillery. High heels, boots, condoms, and tampons were shot from large syringe guns. As time went on, I discovered that relationships at TERROS followed a script similar to daytime soap operas.

All of the arguing drove Steve, Tori, and me to work our next shift at the Tempe House. Unit two, the green van, was now equipped with a radio, lights, and siren. Tori, Steve and I took Unit two to a local drive-in movie and parked in the rear in case of a call from Phoenix. After the movie ended, we returned to the Tempe base. We were bored! Tori was trying to piece together what looked like a paper jigsaw puzzle. This puzzle was actually a letter from her father. Tori explained that her father didn't like to waste paper, so he would write letters on scrap paper, the back of envelopes, and unused sections from other notes and letters, even old checks. Reading a letter from dad was not simply just reading and Tori said it would sometimes take a couple of hours to read his letters from start to finish. She was really happy that he didn't write her very often.

The next afternoon in the Tempe house, Steve and Tori went off duty. Tim and Brian came in as replacements. Tim and I took the ambulance and went to lunch. We decided to return to the Phoenix base to pick up supplies. It was a quiet day in Phoenix. As we drove into the TERROS driveway, we noticed an individual asleep in the front seat of his car. Tim got out of the rig to investigate the car, just in case the guy had overdosed and was unable to come into the house. I sat in the ambulance waiting. Tim turned white, signaled me to drive the ambulance to the other side and park. He ran into the house.

When I casually entered the house, I heard Tim talking to the police. Our sleeper had a grenade in his hand! Within seconds it seemed that every police officer from Phoenix to Mississippi responded. There were armed officers crawling all over the place, inside and out of the house and the grounds. All of us inside the house stood at the windows watching the activity. We certainly did not think about what would happen to us if the grenade exploded.

The sleeper finally woke and found himself surrounded. As he groggily surveyed the situation, he reached into his shirt pocket for a cigarette, placed it between his lips, and casually lifted the grenade. The police raised their guns in anticipation. Tim and I stood at the window facing the car, watching as if it were a dream. The sleeper, with a flick of his thumb, made a small flame pop out of the top and lit his cigarette. The grenade had been converted to a cigarette lighter. The cops holstered their guns and breathed a mass sigh of relief. It put a new light on the "smoking kills" promo. The entry in the com log read:

STARDATE 20, 2135: BOMB LIGHTS UP MARLBORO.

ABOUT THE DRUGS

Amphetamines, cocaine, caffeine, nicotine, and some of the medication used for the treatment of asthma can all be classified as speed. These substances speed up or stimulate the action of the nervous system. Some of the drugs pretend to be the chemicals used by the nerves and brain, while others increase the rate these chemicals are released. The action of caffeine and nicotine pale in comparison to amphetamines and cocaine. Stimulants elevate the blood pressure, heart rate, and respiratory rate. The body becomes tolerant to the effects eventually. Possible consequences of speed use include a stroke or cerebrovascular accident, heart attack, or seizures from the elevation in the blood pressure. These drugs also produce some degree of anorexia, enabling them to be used as diet pills. Even if the user eats, the body will not absorb important nutrients. The physiological responses of the body speed up, prohibiting the absorption of vitamins and other nutrients. Aging processes are also increased. Speed freaks frequently look considerably older than their chronological age. Not only did Ginger appear to be in her sixties, doctors said her internal organs were also functioning as they do in someone in their sixties or seventies.

When loaded, speed freaks speak as though they were a tape on fast forward. We called this a "speed rap." Speed raps are rapid, nonsensical, and repetitive. It was always difficult to understand their speech or even to have a conversation. They pace and move quickly in a non-stop motion. Their hands shake from fine tremors and they can only hold still for approximately three hundredths of a second. Anyone who drinks too much caffeine experiences a similar effect, although much less intense. Staff frequently talked about taking a speed freak home for ten minutes. In that ten minute time span, we figured that a speed freak could completely clean a five bedroom house, including windows, and dig a backyard swimming pool!

The intense amounts of energy are sometimes combined with incredible super-human strength. This strength is similar to our physiological survival phenomenon called the "adrenaline rush or fight or flight." Stories of elderly people lifting a car with one hand while removing their grandchild with the other hand are excellent examples of a "fight or flight." Essentially this survival phenomenon becomes exaggerated in speed freaks.

Any speed obtained from the street tends to be adulterated or "stepped on," commonly with strychnine. In very small concentrations, strychnine has a stimulant action. Aunt Martha's old family recipe calling for a pinch of salt or dash of cinnamon resulted in many variations in taste of the product. What constitutes a pinch of salt or dash of cinnamon varies from individual to individual. In the case of speed, misjudging the ultra-small concentration of strychnine for stimulant effect can result in paralysis of the respiratory system. Sometimes street speed is actually ground up Tedral (for asthma) and at other times the "speed" is actually ANY white powder, including talcum powder. There may be no real drug present at all. But in actuality, this is a problem for any street purchase of any drug. The drug trade is big business and to meet the demand, people will sometimes just sell a variety of powders as the requested drug. We had a client who shot up his "speed," only to find out it was over-the-counter pills containing caffeine (NoDoz). His anxiety attack led to seizures and a stay at the County Hospital.

Chronic use of speed results in the depletion of some brain chemicals. The missing chemicals provide control of the normal emotional state. The combination of malnutrition, lack of sleep, and altered brain chemistry results in violence and paranoid hallucinations.

Classic laboratory experiments have provided evidence for the importance of REM sleep, the rapid eye movement in the dream state, for the maintenance of "normal" emotional balance. People awakened throughout the night by a newborn find themselves in a highly irritable, agitated state due to interruption of their REM sleep. Newborns will periodically allow their parents some sleep.

Speed users, however, are awake several days on end. Then they use downers or sleeping pills to "crash. Unfortunately the majority of downers also suppress the REM sleep, aggravating the violent psychotic outbursts. Speed freaks are notoriously unpredictable; their behavior can rapidly change from relatively calm to violent and out of control. They are unable to explain their behavioral changes. One speed freak we dealt with was shooting at the occupants of a car. He stated that he believed the people were stealing his car. Of course, the occupants were in their own car, not his. Fortunately, he was such a lousy shot that the only thing he hit was a telephone pole.

"Crystal critters" are another aspect speed-induced psychosis. Some users become convinced that some portion of their body is covered by parasites. The user then is obsessed with removing the parasites; however, no one else can see the "critters." In an attempt to remove these parasites one client used his long fingernails to pull his skin away from his arm, exposing muscle and nerves. His arm looked like the drawings in an illustrated medical book, only bloody. Another client carved out craters "filled with critters" using an X-Acto knife. He said, "Pulling them off never worked. They got barbed feet and hang on good!" One client would pour lighter fluid on his arms and light the "critters." While loaded, the client has no pain response and we were the only ones who cringed!

Withdrawal symptoms from speed include insomnia, long periods of sleep, irritability, disorientation, and extreme suicidal obsession. The brain has to replenish its chemical supply, a process that could take up to six months. Probably the best description of withdrawals came from a woman who had been using diet pills prescribed by her physician. She said that she was very happy and she felt very good, except, some portion of her brain seemed to be planning her death! As she faced the mirror each morning, combing her hair and putting on makeup, a voice inside screamed, "SHIT!! YOU'RE STILL ALIVE!!" Sometimes withdrawals can be treated with counseling only. Other times withdrawals are treated with counseling and antidepressant drugs. Once the brain replenishes its supply of chemicals, the individual will have no further problems as long as they do not resume using speed.

Methamphetamine was a legal prescription drug in those days. It was not different from any other form of prescription amphetamines. There were some over-the-counter forms available also. They were used for multiple problems, including appetite control in obesity, hyperkinetic behaviors in children, and to treat narcolepsy. It was also prescribed to people needing to stay awake for long periods of time (truck drivers, college students, etc.). Initially there were no real limits on the quantities available. As reports of abuse and overdoses increased, limits were imposed on the amount that could be obtained legally and approved uses.

Methamphetamine or "Meth" is highly addictive and can be taken orally, smoked as "rock crystal," inhaled, or injected. It is produced from over-the-counter cough and cold medications. Now pharmacies require people to sign logs when they purchase these over-the-counter cough and cold meds as a way for the DEA to monitor large purchases for use in meth labs. The chemical alterations to these drugs produce extremely dangerous vapors. This creates danger to the people in the meth lab and to the neighbors of a meth lab. When police bust a meth lab, everyone involved have to wear a "haz mat" (Hazardous material) suit for protection from the toxic material. These are problems not generally associated with amphetamines.

The effects of meth are similar to amphetamines, although more intense. There is a tendency of meth users to grind their teeth into stubs, called a meth mouth. Sometimes meth users suck on an infant pacifier to relieve the involuntary jaw movements that result in grinding. The body develops tolerance to the anorexia and weight loss associated with both amphetamines and methamphetamines after long term use and the user may eventually gain weight.

Street produced meth now differs from the amphetamines and meth from the seventies in several ways. Withdrawals from amphetamines and meth were much less severe in the seventies than meth now. It was easier for users to remain drug free then. Meth users now desire meth for their life even after they detox. Another rather important difference is that the meth was produced by a reputable pharmaceutical company and the quality was consistent.

In those days we rarely treated anyone for cocaine abuse. Cocaine was relatively pure and cost approximately two thousand dollars per quarter gram. This was much too costly for the majority of people. Generally addicts using street cocaine were actually sniffing some combination of Novocain, baby powder, and amphetamines with less than two percent actual cocaine.

Cocaine is removed from the body very rapidly. When sniffed or snorted, the high lasts approximately five to ten minutes, with a thirty minute afterglow or euphoria. Why, you ask, spend two thousand dollars for a ten minute high? The coke high has been described as better than the best sexual orgasm possible! Let's face it, an orgasm only lasts about ten seconds if you're lucky. We all like to feel good and coke certainly makes the user feel good. The other effects of cocaine are similar to speed, and there is a risk of sudden death with cocaine. Cocaine can create damage to the heart, brain, kidneys, and lungs. Cocaine can be snorted (inhaled), injected, or smoked. People who snort cocaine run the risk of nasal perforation. Cocaine actually impairs sexual function even though the users consider it an aphrodisiac.

Cocaine and its relatives, Novacain and Lidocaine, are not combustible. At some point, some street chemists decided not to snort cocaine because they thought they would have a better high by smoking. In order to be able to smoke cocaine, the combustibility needs to be altered and this process is called freebasing. Essentially, freebasing requires the use of ether to change the combustibility of cocaine so it can be smoked. This process will also remove some of the adulterants. However, ether has a rather nasty habit of exploding, thereby attracting the attention of the police and fire departments.

Some street chemist started using baking soda in place of ether. When the concoction dried, it cracked, thus we have crack cocaine. Now poor quality cocaine, stepped on many times, is available to more people. The quality may be poor but the action is similar in the body. The feelings of power and success provided by the drug are short lived. The user attempts to re-experience the initial feelings. This contributes to making cocaine the hardest drug to kick; after all everyone wants to feel important.

During animal trials of new drugs, it was important to determine if a drug would produce dependency or drug-seeking behaviors. Animals are generally much smarter than humans, they may use some drug introduced by a human, but will not give up food and water to obtain the drug. When humans or lab animals receive cocaine, cocaine stimulates the "reward" center of the brain. This makes the user feel good and creates a powerful craving to continue using the cocaine. Chronic use does lead to tolerance and a decrease in the good feelings, resulting in the user needing to increase their use to try to feel the "old" effects. Withdrawals from cocaine and amphetamines are more psychological than physical. Withdrawals from meth tend to be both psychological and physical.

Chapter 3

Fallin' Out

Opiates

Several weeks after Tim and Sam tried to blow up the fireplace by putting the discarded injectable medications into the fire, I worked with Tori and Jared. It was a very busy, cold night. Tori and I went out to pick up a junk O.D. (heroin overdose). When we returned from the county hospital where we left him, we were freezing. Jared, some Crisis volunteers, and a client or two were asleep in front of the fireplace. All we saw were blankets covering lumps. There was no room in front of the fireplace for us. Necessity, being the mother of invention, sent us into the clinic. We filled a couple of rubber gloves with rubbing alcohol and oxygen and tied them shut. We threw the gloves into the fireplace. When they began exploding, the lumpy blankets moved backward in unison, like giant centipedes moving in reverse. We, the deserving, then took our rightful place in front of the warm fire. The centipedes never woke up until a car pulled up in front of the house, honked, and a body was kicked onto the lawn. We resuscitated the client in a very wet lawn and transported him to the hospital. We returned to the house and renewed our fight over the blankets. As I look back, I am amazed at two things: the fact that the fireplace did not collapse from all the times we exploded things in it and our ability to work together under the enormous stress, save a life, and promptly proceed to bicker like three-year-old children!

When I began working at TERROS, the only therapy for an opiate overdose was supportive care. If the client stopped breathing, we would provide mouth-to-mouth resuscitation; if his/her heart stopped, we performed CPR. There was one drug that could be used, but if the doper had used anything other than an opiate or combined an opiate with anything else, the treatment could be fatal. About a year and a half later we were notified that DuPont had developed a new drug (Narcan or Naloxone) for the treatment of opiate overdoses. We had been selected to participate in the clinical trials of Narcan. Narcan is still considered a superior treatment for opiate overdoses and currently is available by nasal spray, intravenous, intramuscular or subcutaneous injection. It is available to many institutions, including schools.

Mitch, Sam, the doc, and I began to train staff members in injection techniques, dosage, protocol for administration, and the type of medical records to keep. During the final phase of training, someone left a body on our lawn. Everyone ran outside for the "final exam." We placed an airway in the patient's mouth, started mouth-to-mouth resuscitation, took his blood pressure and pulse, and injected Narcan. Within two minutes, he sat up, looked around, leaped to his feet, and ran down the block with our airway still in his mouth. We just stood there until I regained my composure and yelled, "Hey, bring back our airway!" That was the first of many airways we would never saw again.

Celebration of Narcan's actions and passing the "final exam" inspired four male staff members to create a can-can dance and song to extol the virtues of Narcan, ("Narcan can when you can't" sung to the tune of the Can-Can). We had a formal-tie staff party late that night. Everyone had to wear a tie, preferably loud and colorfully decorated, regardless of what else they had on. Most of the male staff were topless with the exception of the tie. Most of the female staff wore t-shirts or the bra section of a bathing suit that clashed with their ties. New relationships were formed at that party. The soap opera love stories continued.

Scheduling of the shifts involved making sure there was always at least one person starting their twenty-four hour shift every twelve hours and at least one person finishing the last twelve hours of their twenty-four hour shift. One day, as Larry and Tori were finishing the first twelve hours of their twenty-four. I was beginning what would turn out to be another educational twenty-four. Tori insisted on spending the evening as dispatcher. She was trying to finish one of those last minute term papers.

Larry was another original staff member, having started at TERROS the same year as Tori. He was very tall, lanky, and almost an albino. He was the "intellectual" and had two claims to fame: he was a fantastic pianist and most staff were hesitant to go on calls when he was the driver. No one would ever explain to the "new kids" why it was preferable not to allow Larry possession of the ignition keys. On those shifts he announced his desire to drive, off-duty staff would leave and the working crew members would fight over the dispatch radio. These were the times that the house sounded like the Muslim call to prayer. I was soon to discover why Larry had this effect on the others.

Our first call of the shift was a very quiet, mellow code two transport. We had to take a puppy to the emergency vet. Rover had ingested some of his owner's speed. At least the puppy didn't attack the stop light. After we dropped Rover and his parent at the vet, Larry and I were cleaning the back of the ambulance. This was standard protocol regardless of the species of patient.

Larry and I were scrubbing the inside of the van and chatting. This was our first shift together. At that moment Tori radioed that we had an overdose on the other side of town. I tossed the gurney and equipment into the van to finish cleaning. Larry slammed the doors and ran to the front. He started the engine, radioed acknowledgement of the call, and turned on the lights and siren As we took off, I noticed that it was slightly more difficult maintaining my balance while I was cleaning, but I rationalized that traffic may have been heavier than usual.

When I finished cleaning, I crawled forward to the shotgun seat. I was sorry that I did. Larry was driving down the sidewalk on the wrong side of the street! As I noticed this rather strange driving pattern, I began to regret having no will. I was so terrified that my hand continually slipped from the wail to the yelp buttons on the siren, and our siren sounded like a hysterical monkey or Jimi Hendrix playing an electric guitar. We had to turn right, which meant departing from the sidewalk, traversing eight lanes of heavy traffic and attempting to avoid the eighteen-wheeler in the middle of the cross street. Larry cut through a gas station and almost removed one of the pumps. From that moment, until we arrived at the scene, I rode on the floor under the dashboard. My heartbeat was so loud that I couldn't hear the siren or the radio.

Incredibly, we arrived safely and entered the house. We were escorted into the kitchen to an unconscious female by the man who had called in the overdose (the reporting party). I began recording the blood pressure and other vital signs, while Larry began mouth-to-mouth resuscitation. As I prepared to inject the Narcan, I noticed that Larry had a frightened look on his face. Larry was the proverbial "white as a sheet," although this was difficult for an albino, and his eyes were bugging out of his head. The client recovered and we monitored her for two hours at the house.

As we were talking to the client and her friend, Larry casually asked the client's male friend, "Why were you holding the gun?"

My mouth dropped open and I began babbling, "*Whaaaat* gun?" No one paid any attention to my babblings. The friend nonchalantly responded, "If my woman died, so did yours." Now *I was the white sheet!* All the way back to TERROS, I trembled and sweated, my body attempting to relieve itself of the "adrenaline rush." I'm not sure what was more exciting and frightening, the code three ride or discovery of the gun at the back of my head. I didn't sleep at all during that twenty-four hour shift.

One evening, we picked up an overdose and brought him back to TERROS to monitor. He initially responded to the simple tilt of the head and pinch of his sternum. Every time he nodded, we kicked him in the knees and screamed, "Breathe stupid!" He bolted upright, scratched, and had a look of astonishment and said, "What do you mean breathe? Man, I was breathin', I always breathe." (Scratch, scratch, nod).

"You're noddin'." (Kick, scream).

"I wasn't noddin'." (Scratch, scratch). "I was examining my eyelids for light leaks."

In the vernacular of the street, a junkie who nods and turns blue has "fallen out."

The first time I was dispatched to a person who had "fallen out," I spent the entire trip operating the sirens, navigating and worrying about the possibilities. Since I was unfamiliar with the terminology I wondered, "had the individual fallen out of a speeding train? A tall building? A moving car? An airplane passing overhead?"

Would I need a body bag or dust pan to collect the pieces? Did we have enough splints? It was almost anticlimactic to arrive at the residence of someone needing only a reminder to breathe.

When a junkie nods around well-intentioned friends, their problems are intensified. Street methods of resuscitation, before calling for help, do not even closely resemble the methods taught by the Heart Association or the Red Cross. Street "Thump Therapy" complicates the job of the medical personnel and alters the survival possibilities of the user. This treatment mode includes ice, milk, and salt water.

The rescuer will pack the scrotum or breast of the overdosed individual in ice. This results in frostbite of some rather personal parts and a loud banging noise if someone tries to help a male junkie walk before all the ice packed around the scrotum is melted. With large quantities of ice, the rescuer will put their friend in a bathtub and pile ice on top. I think some people believe that the gills an embryo has during early development will resume function in an adult. The drop in body temperature is so extreme that there have been many instances of people being pronounced dead by some emergency room physician after several attempts at resuscitation. The body is then covered by a blanket and the paperwork filled out.

As a child we all heard about the miracles obtained from a glass of milk, another favorite resuscitation method involves injecting milk into the vein. This is not only very painful, but causes the risk of fat emboli (blood clots). We had one o.d. treated with powdered milk mixed with bourbon. Unfortunately this "treatment" did not save him, but the Narcan did. He had some ugly scars from the injection site of the milk. He was very ill from the injected bourbon and powdered milk and spent a couple of days in the hospital. These little clots plug up the blood vessels as they travel through the body. Sometimes there is no milk, so the rescuer reaches for salt.

Table salt is poured into a glass with water. It is stirred and more salt added until a layer of salt approximately one inch thick is on the bottom of the glass, indicating a supersaturated solution. This is then injected into the muscle, resulting in very severe pain, injury to the tissues and abscesses.

I believe that these street "treatments" are considered successful because the user responds to the painful stimulus. We perform a similar method by the sternal rub (rubbing the sternum or breastplate with a great deal of force). When a person yells in pain they are forced to breathe.

My favorite street therapy is mouth-to-mouth performed by fist meeting mouth. Our ambulance dispatcher would very carefully describe how to perform mouth to mouth resuscitation, the type approved by the Heart Association and Red Cross. Speaking rapidly dispatch would say,

"Take a deep breath and place your mouth (the hole between the nose and chin containing teeth and tongue) on your friend's mouth—also a hole containing teeth and tongue. Blow in the air, watch for the chest to rise. Then remove your mouth—the thing containing teeth and tongue. Allow your friend to blow the air out and then repeat . . ." (pant, pant).

Although this seemed pretty clear and we tried to include all details for the steps, we would frequently find the "rescuer" punching the overdosed individual in the face, yelling "Breathe!" We spent considerable time evaluating the instructions for any term that even remotely sounded like, "Take your fist and hit your friend in the face with as much force as possible." A variation of this method was for the rescuer to jump up and down on the victim's chest, smashing the rib cage and damaging the heart, lungs, and liver and spleen.

One man picked up his overdosed girlfriend, whined, "Honey, please breathe. Why ain't you breathing?"

Then he dropped her. He leaned down, picked her up, and repeated the process until we arrived. I would always hope that the overdosed individual had no friends to help, thereby allowing us the chance to perform a more acceptable form of mouth-to-mouth resuscitation.

An additional problem faced by junkies is the material used to step on, or cut the drugs. Pure heroin is actually white with a bitter taste. Heroin is usually only one to twenty percent pure, depending on where you buy and how much you can pay. In other words, a gram of heroin actually contains only one hundredth to two tenths gram of heroin and the remainder is garbage, increasing the profit of the seller. Common cutting agents include coffee, tar, chocolate, quinine, milk sugar (lactose), brown sugar, starch, and foot powder or baby powder. Black tar heroin is sticky black like roofing tar or coal. It usually comes from Mexico and the components are not consistent.

At one time, there was a batch of heroin containing eighty-five percent Coumadin (Warfarin) on the streets for a brief period of time. Coumadin is a blood thinner related to rat poison. When people take this drug under their physician's supervision, they have frequent blood tests to ensure that the dose is not too high, which could result in hemorrhage from all body regions. The junkies were not aware of the presence of this chemical and several people bled to death. Homicide detectives contacted us for information to help track down the individual responsible for "steppin' heavy." I don't think the chemist really wanted to kill the users, but was just trying to increase their profit and probably didn't have any foot powder available.

Dealers would occasionally try to "hot shot" a junkie if they suspect that the junkie was cooperating with police, associating with someone the dealer doesn't like, or if the junkie was late paying the bill. A hot shot usually consisted of heroin laced with battery acid, arsenic, or some other equally wonderful chemical. A hot shot was designed to kill the user. The presence of Coumadin in the heroin was not designed to be a hot shot because the dope was not sold to just one or two specific users.

Although TV shows generally portray a junkie as violent, they are usually too busy scratching and nodding to be aggressive. Many are gainfully employed in legitimate business. Those involved in criminal activities to obtain their supply were hookers or rob unoccupied residences. Violence during withdrawals doesn't resemble the TV version either. Symptoms of opiate withdrawals are similar to the flu. The most violence exhibited during a bout of the flu is to throw oneself onto a toilet seat! Occasionally, one might hurtle the empty toilet paper cardboard at a wall. This violent vomiting and diarrhea can last five to seven days.

There have been many treatment methods advocated for opiate withdrawals. We were involved in a double-blind research experiment for outpatient opiate detox using Darvon-N. All of our detox clients would come to TERROS daily for medication and counseling. Rules for participating in detox were strictly enforced, focusing responsibility on the individual. Clients late for their appointment with the Detox Counselor would have to wait until the next day to receive their medications.

Junkies are probably the greatest con artists on the face of the earth and they tend to blame others for their problems. There was always a good excuse for being late. Unfortunately for the junkie, the Detox staff was not swayed by these great excuses. Eventually we made a large wheel with all of the common excuses written on it. We attached a spinner, allowing the client to play "Spin an Excuse." The only things missing were the commercials, sexy host or hostess, theme music, and voice-over announcing the prizes.

It was amazing how many times a person was late because their grandmother or mother died or they had a flat tire. Generally Crisis staff was not affected by the detox clients wandering in, unless the person stood in front of the TV. Detox clients would occasionally whine at everyone, especially the Crisis staff while waiting for their counselor. We would spin the wheel for them so they would be prepared with excuses for their counselor. The major exception to Crisis staff being affected by detox was when a detox client shot herself in the head while talking to her counselor. I was on vacation and was not too unhappy about missing the mess and excitement.

One of our neighbors was a very tall man with a small head. He resembled "Baby Huey" from the cartoons. Baby Huey was one of those people who would take any drug he could get his hands on. He had no particular preference of drugs. He would come to the house and borrow quarters from on-duty staff and volunteers. If he liked a person, he would demonstrate his affection by pulling out hunks of hair from the subject of his admiration.

One hot afternoon, Baby Huey skated into the house on roller skates. He was wearing an oversized suit from Goodwill and had shaved his head. Skating around the living room, a difficult feat considering the semi-shag carpeting, he asked for money. Since most of the staff had hair pulled out at some point, everyone suddenly became deaf and dumb to his presence. Hairless Mr. Clean gave

Baby Huey a dollar and told him, "Never return this money when I am in the house."

Baby Huey grinned and skated out. There was a vigorous round of applause because we knew he would avoid Mr. Clean. Everyone would now want to work shifts with Mr. Clean to avoid Baby Huey. Scheduling crisis shifts was about to become a nightmare and another source of fighting among staff.

According to the house rumor, Mr. Clean stood in front of bars at night, grinning and holding out his hand. Supposedly he would reach out asking for a dollar as people walked by! His appearance was so ominous; people gave him all their cash and offered their spouse as collateral. Well, you know how rumors are. Maybe that is why he never cashed his paychecks.

Within a few minutes of Baby Huey's exit, Karen and I left for an opiate overdose. As we drove out hot (with lights and siren, code three), we passed Baby Huey skating down the street. Law requires emergency vehicles to stop at red lights before "breaking traffic" (crossing the intersection). This protects those people not paying attention or driving with windows up and radio at full blast. Karen and I stopped at the intersection and were preparing to break traffic when Baby Huey caught up to us. He was so mad that we stopped at the intersection that he began beating on the van. No one knows why he created those dents, maybe because the van was hairless? Baby Huey kept trying to keep up with us but couldn't skate fast enough.

About a couple of miles further on we had a flat tire. Karen calmly radioed in, got Alice (the med box) and the oxygen, and we began to hitchhike to the call. It was obvious that this was not the first time she had this problem. As time went along, it was not the only time I was to face this situation. Standing by a disabled ambulance and trying to thumb a ride was very humiliating, especially when we were passed by. I think Baby Huey probably passed us up too. Eventually, we made it to the call. It was a game (false) call.

Some days it doesn't pay to get out of bed! We thumbed another ride to the ambulance, changed the tire, and returned to the house. I was glad that I only had nine hours left on my shift. The next series of cartoons showed Karen and I seductively waving the oxygen, and Alice, at passing cars. In one frame, the oxygen tank was offered fifty dollars for sexual favors. About two a.m. that same night, Jared and I went to an all-night restaurant. As we were finishing our breakfast, a car failed to negotiate a slight curve on the street. The car came through the windows at the restaurant and parked on one of the tables about four seats from us. There were about fifteen people in the restaurant when it became a parking lot. Everyone was screaming or crying, but the uninjured helped those injured or pinned.

We radioed for assistance and Jared ran out to get Alice, backboards, and the gurney from the ambulance. I began assisting the driver and victims. Jared returned with the equipment, but he had a strange look on his face. The police, fire, and another ambulance arrived to assist. Fortunately no one was seriously injured, although everyone was transported to local hospitals. As we went out to our ambulance with our patients, I realized why Jared had that look. The car had scraped the side of our unit and removed the roof of the car next to us. By the time we had tended to everything, I had one hour left both on my shift *and* to live after all the damage to the new rig was accounted for.

My next shift, Steve, Tori, and I were working at the Tempe house. It was a very quiet night so Steve rolled over on the floor and dialed the phone very quietly as Tori was concentrating on her homework. Tori answered the phone, not paying attention to the fact that the other light was lit. Suddenly, she made a very strange face. I was trying to listen to both conversations. Steve was telling Tori that he had a bad habit (addiction), and that he was mainlining marshmallows into his vein. For thirty minutes, she tried to counsel the client on his problem. Tori wrote me a note about the conversation. I wrote back, "giant or miniature?" When I could no longer contain my laughter, Tori realized who her client was and she began yelling at Steve through the phone receiver. She was too angry to notice that he had replaced his receiver and was no longer in the room. By that time I was laughing so hard that tears were streaming down my cheeks.

After working ten years in hospitals, I thought that I had seen everything. I found that I was no longer amazed at what people did to themselves. At times I would be still surprised, but no longer amazed. There are people who get a high from the act of an injection and not from the substance they are injecting. These needle freaks would shoot anything just for that high. Among the hazards of injecting drugs without proper training or using dirty needles is cotton poisoning. Cotton poisoning is the result of injecting a small amount of solid substance into veins. The solid material excites the platelets in the blood stream. Platelets are sticky and clump together with the red blood cells to form clots in the blood vessels. The clots plug up the smaller blood vessels or travel to the lungs or the brain.

The term cotton poisoning originally came from filtering the last bit of heroin through a cigarette filter to "clean it." The user would then squeeze out the drug and inject it. We had clients who would reuse syringe needles and when the needle would get dull, they would rub it in Crisco oil or butter. Sometimes they would rub the needle on their pants or shirt to "clean" it.

We treated many cases of cotton poisoning at TERROS and the clients usually required hospitalization. The people would develop a high fever, muscle cramps, and joint pains almost immediately after the solid substance entered their veins. Steve may have been joking when he called about his habit of shooting marshmallows, but we did treat a man who had shot peanut butter. He was far too ill for me to satisfy my curiosity. I was dying to know if he planned to inject bread and jam to make a sandwich the hard way. I even resisted the urge to ask as to whether it was crunchy or smooth. He almost died from the clots.

ABOUT THE DRUGS

Opiates (also known as opioids), such as heroin, Percodan, codeine, Darvon, and Morphine, are used medically to relieve pain, cough, and diarrhea. Technically, opiates are derived from opium. These include morphine, codeine, heroin, and opium. Opioids are synthetic drugs manufactured to act in a similar fashion on the same opioid brain receptors. Examples of opioids are Methadone, Percodan, OxyContin, Vicodin, Demerol, and Fentanyl. Essentially these drugs don't actually stop the pain, but, rather, keep the brain from recognizing it.

The drugs open all the small blood vessels in the skin by causing the release of histamine. This produces the same effect as having a runny nose while rolling in poison oak wearing long woolen underwear! Watching someone scratch and rub their nose with that intensity is much worse than watching someone yawn! Soon you find yourself scratching with the same enthusiasm. Opiates cause the pupils (the center of the eye) to constrict to pinpoint size. Pupils constrict in bright light to protect the retina in the back of the eye. Normally the pupils dilate in dim light. The pupils of an opiate user remain pinned regardless of the lighting conditions. This can cause problems in users outdoors during the day.

Chronic opiate use will also cause the blood sugar to drop. Junkies tend to be constipated, crave sugar, and use a lot of Preparation H! When we would go to eat at three or four a.m., we could always pick out the junkies in the restaurant. They would sit at the counter and order pie ala mode and coffee. As they pour sugar into the coffee, they scratch and nod. Eventually, a mound of sugar would become visible above the brim of the cup. They would then drink this concoction and eat their pie ala mode followed by a candy bar. Opiate addicts are a dentist's delight; you could actually hear the teeth yelling for help!

Added to this assortment of symptoms is the junkie nod. Ever been around someone recently out of surgery? They begin a conversation and fade off into la-la land before the words are completely past their lips. Hours later they resume the conversation as though there had been no time gap. Junkies are the same type of conversationalist. During a nod, junkies also tend to allow their head to fall forward. This position makes breathing difficult for anyone. It is especially difficult when loaded on a drug that selectively inactivates the automatic reflexes controlling respiration.

People rarely think about breathing, unless they are trying to attract attention by heavy breathing, or someone is listening to their lung sounds with a stethoscope. As you are reading this, you may become aware of your respiratory rate and may even be overriding your automatic control in an effort to change it. However, once your attention is no longer focused on your lung action, the automatic reflexes resume and corrections are made. If you try to override the system too long, you pass out. Monitors in the large arteries notify your brain and lungs of the necessary corrective measures and you return to normal.

High levels of opiates essentially short circuit this involuntary system. People literally need to be reminded to inhale and exhale. During the nod, they forget to breathe, turn blue (cyanotic), and are likely to die. Frequently the only treatment needed is to push the head up, opening the trachea (windpipe), and providing a slight painful stimulus to cause the person to take a deep breath. Maintaining a respiratory rate could then be accomplished by engaging in some type of verbal argument with the client or preventing them from nodding by kicking them in the shins each time they nodded.

In 2016, as of the writing of this book, there is an opioid epidemic in the United States. I do not know what is causing this increased use, primarily among young upper and middle class adults, and why there is such a high rate of deaths. Part of the problem seems to be from counterfeit Fentanyl patches. Fentanyl comes as a patch (similar to nicotine patches) for the treatment of severe and chronic pain. It was designed for transdermal use and the medication is released over seventy-two hours. I have heard of people cutting open the patch and sucking out the medication. The misuse of the Fentanyl combined with it being manufactured in "shady" labs has definitely increased the number of deaths. At this time, some schools are applying for permission to stock Narcan. Narcan has been available to First Responders since about 1974.

Chapter 4

Gettin' Down

Depressant Drugs, Downers

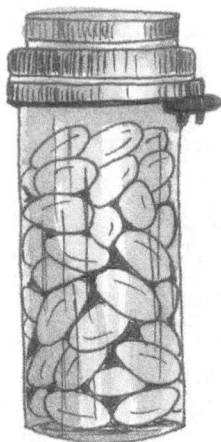

One evening, about eight thirty p.m., Tim and I and two volunteers, responded code three to an unknown overdose. The caller became concerned about her friend, an elderly woman, and broke into the apartment. She found her unconscious, with shallow respirations. A large punch bowl, filled with pills, was on the bedside table. The neighbor suspected a possible overdose because of the pills and the friend's most recent statements. We brought in our book with pictures of almost all prescribed medications. Tim was administering oxygen and an IV, while I was trying to identify the drugs and talk to the hospital and our doctor. The volunteers brought in the gurney.

There were pills for high blood pressure, digitalis for the heart, and iron for anemia. Some of the pills were sedatives (downers) for insomnia or anxiety. Others were vitamins, over-the-counter allergy tabs, pain pills, and aspirin. A large number of pills were not easily identified. We received orders from our doctor to begin an IV and administer Narcan. We transported the woman to the hospital code three, along with her punch bowl. En route she coded (her heart stopped) and I initiated CPR.

We had to cross railroad tracks to reach the hospital. As we approached the tracks, the guard arms came down stopping us. There were railroad personnel standing by the tracks. Tim used the loudspeaker to request that the railroad workers signal the train to slow or somehow allow us across. The workers either didn't hear, due to the sirens and clanging crossing alarm, or they were choosing to ignore us. Unfortunately when the train arrived, it began slowly moving forward and back on the tracks. Tim said it looked like it was loading a car or changing tracks or . . . I was impressed that Tim was able to weigh his words carefully when radioing the situation to the hospital and our base. The word was that the FCC (Federal Communications Commission) monitored communications and could pull our license for offensive language. We really didn't know whether to believe that or not, but no one was willing to risk it.

The siren and the railroad warning bell were giving me a headache. The railroad personnel were ignoring our siren, so Tim shut it off and crawled into the back to assist me in administering CPR while the train continued to block traffic. It seemed like six months before the tracks were clear and we could continue. The woman's heart resumed beating as we arrived at the hospital. Once we turned her care over to the hospital staff, I felt as though I had just played racquetball for three hours! CPR is probably the most exhausting activity an individual can participate in, even if there is a "Code Team" like in hospitals.

One of our other downer freak cases overdosed just prior to labor. According to her friends, she was beginning to have labor pains just as she ingested a large quantity of pills. By the time we were notified and arrived on the scene, she was unconscious and the baby's head was showing (crowning). We were not only attempting to keep the mother alive, but we had to deliver the baby without the mom's pushing. We couldn't transport because the baby had crowned, but we couldn't stay because the mom was overdosed. Now, that's what is meant as caught between a rock and a hard place! The baby was almost as "downed out" as mom, his initial respirations were very shallow and his muscle tone was limp. We almost lost both mother and baby but they were finally stabilized for transport to the hospital. We received word a couple of nights later that mom and child were in withdrawal but the prognosis was good.

I spent one lovely spring afternoon on the phone with a young man named George who was combining alcohol and barbiturates. A combination of drug categories often assures an overdose and probably death. George said he wanted to talk to someone while "dying." He told me what he was taking as he swallowed the pills or the booze.

"Well, there goes another four reds and (gulp) Jim Beam." Reds are the street name for Secobarbitol.

I managed to get his address and dispatch the ambulance. When he saw them pull up through his living room window, he was very upset.

"What the hell are they doing here?" he yelled at me.

"Who are you talking about?" I asked in a very stunned voice.

"Damned people in an ambulance that's who!"

I acted as if I was shocked. "As long as they are there, could you let them in? I need to give them a phone message."

"Yea, ok, but they can't stop me from drinking!"

The ambulance crew knew that I had to be sneaky about them coming so they played along. George allowed them in. I heard him banging into the walls and furniture as he walked to the door. The crew keyed the mic (microphone) so that I could monitor their conversation and keep the hospital informed during transport. George was initially uncoordinated and his speech slurred but he became more and more agitated. At one point George swung at Jason and threatened to rearrange Sam's anatomy. He refused treatment and transport. George then fell, began convulsing and stopped breathing, giving us "implied consent" for transport. The crew initiated CPR and transported to the nearest hospital code three. The hospital pumped George's stomach, admitted him to ICU in critical condition and sutured Jason's head.

One evening, after the volunteers left and Crisis was quiet, I was snoozing on the couch in the living room, ignoring the various lice and etc. inhabiting the cushions. Tim was asleep in the back room with the hospital bed and Tori was sleeping in the second bedroom. About four a.m. we received a call about a possible overdose. Tim and I left for the address. We woke Tori to work the phones. When we arrived at the address we saw four VERY LOADED people staring at a body on the floor. Tim and I prepared to start CPR and place an IV line in. Then we realized the client was very, very dead and in rigor mortis. He was as stiff as a two-by-four board. We asked about when the guy collapsed.

"How long has he been down man?" Tim asked.

"He went down about my third hit, man," one guy said.

"NO, man, it was when I went to pee," another helpful soul said.

"You gotta help him, man," a very large bulky man said in a threatening voice. He had a noticeable bulge in his pants that resembled a gun.

We decided to pretend to do CPR, which was difficult on someone so stiff. We loaded him into the ambulance, radioed Tori, and headed for the hospital. Tori radioed us before we left the hospital and said that she had been receiving calls from people at the party about their friend. She only told them that the name of the hospital their friend was at. We decided the police could fill in the details.

A few weeks later, Tim and I responded to a barbiturate overdose in an apartment complex surrounded by trees. The fire department was first on the scene and called us. We evaluated the patient and decided to transport to the hospital for monitoring. Mud and the outside design of the apartment complex were going to interfere with the safe movement of a gurney, so we decided that I would back the ambulance close to the doorway for easier loading of the gurney. A fireman on the scene was directing me around the trees. He failed to notice an ambulance eating branch. I was watching his hand signals and didn't suspect anything until the blue gumball was sheared almost completely off. We loaded the client into the ambulance and I jumped in the back with him to monitor and radio information to the hospital.

Meanwhile, Tim climbed up and used Kerlex gauze to reconnect the gumball to the light bar. En route to the hospital code three, we were delayed by a slow moving vehicle in front of us. The driver was not responding to the sirens, so Tim picked up the loudspeaker microphone and yelled, "Move to the right!" The driver continued in front of us for a few seconds, then drove across oncoming traffic and parked on the sidewalk. Tim and I decided that we would have to be more specific as to which right from that point on. We left the client at the hospital and returned to base for the staff meeting.

By this time, the gumballs had been removed several times and there were several scratches and dings in the ambulance, so we weren't in as much trouble. The staff cartoonist drew a cartoon showing the gumball wearing a cast and supported by crutches.

The Tempe house was rarely very busy. It became a place to go to relax and get paid. The Board of Directors decided to close the Tempe crisis house and rent another building in Tempe for training staff and volunteers. Sam and Tom bought a mannequin with artificial "veins and blood" to be used for training the staff on intravenous medication techniques. According to the directions the "blood" that came with the IV mannequin would only stain wool. We discovered, the hard way, that something was lost in the translation from Chinese and the "blood" stained everything except wool. Our bright red hands and clothes were the telltale signs that we had just completed a training session on injection techniques. We took both of the training mannequins, a donated camera, and a VCR to Tempe. The administrative staff upstairs was delighted that they would no longer have to worry about finding a mannequin in their closet or under their desk.

Staff taped a series of training videos covering all aspects of the Basic Drug Abuse Technician for training volunteers. We had so much fun with our movie debut that we also taped our own versions of "*Star Trek*" and "*M*A*S*H*." Our versions weren't acceptable for family viewing; however, watching them did brighten up the down hours especially between three and four-thirty a.m. Some of our more prudish volunteers would hide their faces, trying to avoid watching.

With all of the equipment used for training stored at the Tempe house, we once again began changing the rooms at the Phoenix house. The room on the east side of the hallway, nearest the bathroom, was turned into an office for Sam, the Training Coordinator. The room next to Sam's office, located directly behind the living room wall, became a staff lounge. No one ever lounged in there and this room eventually set off the "TV war."

Someone decided to remove the slanted wall that had been put up between crisis and outpatient detox. A small laboratory was set up near the clinic enabling the doctors to do simple microscopic exams. The anteroom was divided into a small room to greet people as they walked in and a larger crisis clinic. We had obtained a large hospital exam table and new cabinets stocked with our emergency medications. The new wall facing the anteroom was covered with cork and was frequently mistaken for a dartboard. We removed the crab-infested, flattened, black-grey carpeting from the floor of the crisis clinic and replaced it with linoleum. Somewhere there must be an adage: When Bored, Build, and Then Rebuild It in a Novel Way.

As the new training center became a reality, new relationships began to grow as well. As I said, relationships at TERROS frequently reminded me of TV soap operas. Mitch and Linda announced their engagement. Linda was a crisis staff member involved in an earlier break up. Steve and "Hot Lips" decided that they would live together. Sam and Karen were considering marriage. Suddenly, it seemed as if an epidemic of wedding bells was beginning.

About four months after the Tempe training house opened, a major fire occurred in the adjacent building. We notified all of our off-duty staff to come help get the equipment from the building. Steve and Tom arrived, ran inside the building, and carried out the mannequins. They casually tossed them in the back of Steve's pickup. Some of the "blood" was dripping from the veins of our IV mannequin.

Sam and Carla carried out the carpet, VCR, and tapes. Steve was preparing to drive off when he was stopped by the police. They attempted to arrest him for concealing a dead or dying body. Using life-sized training mannequins was definitely a hassle, especially when they bleed. He was stopped several times during the trip back to the Phoenix house. I really was curious about the thoughts of the people driving past Steve's truck.

"Did anyone run off the road as a truck with bodies went past?" I wondered. Cell phones were not available and so we speculated that passing motorists were asking questions such as: "Where is the nearest telephone booth?" "Do the cops know?" A couple of us tried to predict how many calls the police received about the truck with the dead guys going from Tempe to Phoenix.

I began conducting more of the training sessions for the staff and volunteers. Sam was starting his training as a Physician's Assistant and resigned as the Training Coordinator. I was officially promoted and eventually became the official Training Coordinator, as an adjunct to my Crisis Headstaff position. We began receiving requests for training from businesses and agencies in other states. My academic program began competing with my Crisis shifts and training sessions at TERROS and around the state. I probably would have quit school but my major professor managed to convince me to stay and finish my degree.

The volunteers and new staff were required to attend "Basic Drug Abuse Technician" training and work shifts as observers until they completed the courses. Staff was required to attend the "Advanced Drug Abuse Technician" classes which included training in medication use. When the state started the Paramedic program, we were allowed to challenge the exams and most of us received our licenses as paramedic.

Now that the training mannequins were back in the Phoenix house following the fire in Tempe, a new game of "Find the Dummy" began. Mannequins sometimes could be found on the gurney in the ambulance, assuming the rig was not out on a call at shift change. Occasionally a mannequin would be left in the bathroom for some unsuspecting desperate soul who planned on sitting on the toilet alone. Sometimes Tom would find a mannequin hanging in effigy in his office or in the living room, especially when he established some policy we considered unacceptable and off the wall. Now that I think of it, Tom frequently dreamed up some off the wall policy that made most of us angry. I remember we once decapitated the mannequin and left the head in Tom's desk drawer. Almost as effective as the horse's head scene in the *Godfather* movie! I think his shriek was heard all the way to Tucson, about a hundred and twenty miles away.

ABOUT THE DRUGS

Downers include alcohol, anti-anxiety, anticonvulsants, muscle relaxants, and sleeping pills. There are thousands of drugs in this group, barbiturates, Valium, and Quaaludes represent just a small portion of them. These drugs randomly depress any energy using cell. As the level of drug in the brain increases, the brain function decreases. Initially there is a relaxed, warm, giddy feeling. Motor functions are affected, manifested by incoordination, and the user finds walking to be a new adventure. Loss of inhibitions results in inappropriate or violent behavior. People say whatever pops into their mind without regard to the sentence content, social setting, or status of the listener. Downer freaks and alcoholics often attempt to rearrange the anatomy of someone, usually due to loss of inhibitions. Speech becomes slurred as the drug levels increase in the brain.

There may be seizures, unconsciousness, and even death may occur. Many downer freaks simply enjoy sitting in the corner drooling on themselves.

Most people have heard about the DTs (delirium tremens) of alcohol withdrawals. Patients have altered mental status and hyperactivity which can progress to cardiovascular collapse and death. Detox from other depressants can result in similar problems such as high temperature, seizures, hallucinations, and agitation. Unfortunately, the withdrawals may also lead to status epilepticus, a non-stop seizure. Status epilepticus from depressant withdrawals is frequently fatal. Depressant withdrawals are not as simple to treat as opiate withdrawals. Depressant withdrawal cases were generally admitted to the hospital for a two week stay.

It was always interesting when we would transport an alcoholic to the local detox center. One client described a naked belly dancer under the gurney. He hung over the edge of the gurney and provided a full detailed description of the "dancer." "Damn she is really pretty with long black hair. She gots (sic) a really shiny rock, hmmm, maybe a diamond, in her belly button. She gots (sic) just a purple and blue bra but it's too small and her boobs are hanging out and bouncing. She gots (sic) a pretty pair of underpants on that are green. They look like they could cause a major wedgie. She gots (sic) no shoes but yellow socks. Swear she must be about twenty. She is waving her hips in all directions. She got smacked in the face by her big boob! Look at her go!"

Chapter 5

Disregarding Sanity

A Multitude of Problems

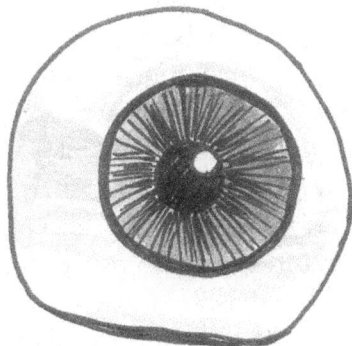

Tim and I had gone to our favorite Mexican restaurant when Tori dispatched us code two (no lights or sirens) back to the house. After approximately three minutes, we were notified to switch to code three. My ride with Larry was always fresh in my memory when a male staff member was driving and I started to get on the floor. We arrived at the house without once driving along the sidewalk! As we walked toward the house, we heard the unmistakable sound of a gunshot. Tim and I rolled onto the grass, crouched down, and slowly continued toward the house. Tim's Vietnam experiences taught him how to traverse through gunfire, and I followed his lead. We cautiously approached the house and entered the crisis counseling door by sidling in.

The phone was off the hook and the voice at the other end was screaming, "Hello, hello!" Tim picked up the receiver and discovered someone calling about drug identification. She said she was talking to Tori, heard the door slam, and voices in the background. She said that Tori said she would look up the drug identification and call her back. Just then she heard a loud male voice and Tori put the receiver down, but not on the phone cradle. We were worried about Tori and the gunshot.

Tori came into the room and was as white as a sheet. She explained that she had been doing a suicide rap with the person at the time when the phone rang. She told the visiting client that she had to take the phone call and would be right back to him. He excused himself to the bathroom. We hung up the phone and carefully looked around. We found Tori's client in the bathroom. He had shot himself in the head. Apparently he had started a suicide note before coming to TERROS and then added an addendum with an apology to Tori. By the time we finished with the police, coroner, and our Medical Director, Tim and Tori were ready to go off-duty and I was ready to resign.

David was called in and he came to meet us at the house. He helped us talk through the events and our feelings. Tim had talked to David immediately after we radioed what had happened and requested the authorities. If David hadn't been there to help, I would have never worked another day at TERROS. It was important that we all understood not everyone could be helped to end their misery, without ending their life. I came to TERROS to help people and had a hard time understanding that sometimes help didn't mean making all the bad things go away.

I was not upset about death, after all, I had worked in hospitals for many years and death was always just a part of life. Death by your own hands was a different story. I have felt very low and depressed many times but I never considered ending my own life, especially by such a violent means.

I was still depressed and mentally evaluating the recent suicide events when my shift was about to end. Off-duty staff had heard about the incident and almost everyone came in to express their concerns. Tori stopped by to continue talking to David. Everyone sat in front of the TV, lost in their thought and there was little conversation. An older man walked in and asked us to call him a cab. Under other circumstances someone would have responded, "Ok, you're a cab." While the man was waiting for the cab, he commented on the number of people trying to watch a nine-inch black-and-white TV. As he left he said, "I will buy you a real TV." No one believed it until an eighteen-inch color console TV arrived a couple of days later. That was one very expensive cab ride!

My next shift started by "Hot Lips" the comptroller yelling that I had to take at least one week of my vacation time or I would lose it. One of the new volunteers ran screaming through the house because the mannequin was hanging in the bathroom with a size forty-two DD bra wrapped around its neck. Two of the Detox staff were fighting over fouled up paperwork. Even Christmas created problems. The tree was placed by the fireplace, and then moved by the front door. There was the fireplace group and the front door group arguing. If someone from the fireplace group was in the ambulance with the door group, the argument took place all the way to and from the call. No place like home!

After the staff meeting that day, most of the staff were sitting and discussing recent events, especially the death of Tori's suicide rap. Death was not a new aspect of our business, and we all had talked with suicidal people on the phone and in person. Usually we were able to convince the person to seek counseling, but we were all aware that the same thing could happen to us that had happened to Tori. Sometimes people would attempt to make us responsible for their inability to find value in life. We were trying to find ways to take care of ourselves when we couldn't fix things for someone else.

During this brainstorming session about responsibility, a young man walked in wearing a long raincoat. Although it was early winter, the temperature outside was in the high eighties and the monsoon season hadn't started yet. Rain was definitely not in the picture. The man politely greeted the female staff and started flashing the male staff. The women began roaring with laughter. The males became infuriated. One of the men called the police. The women accused the guys of overreacting. After all, the men thought it was funny when the women received obscene phone calls. When the police arrived to escort the flasher off of the property, he flashed the police! They didn't see the humor in it either. Another unexpected form of comic relief had just entered our life at just the right time.

CONCERTS

Early in 1974, a major rock concert promoter had decided to hold outdoor summer concerts in Tempe. He contracted with another ambulance agency and us to supply medical backup at these concerts. The other ambulance company attended with "Big Bertha," a rig about the size of a large Winnebago, containing the equivalent of a small hospital surgical unit. The crews from this company were dressed in blues with silver badges, close enough to the police uniforms to discourage requests for assistance from most of those attending the concert. Both agencies would receive payment for the ambulances, medications, and staff time.

The staff working the concert would see a free show if not busy, meet the entertainers, and get paid overtime. We worked concerts for several years and saw some of the principal groups of the time: Edgar Winters; War; Crosby, Stills, Nash and Young. Everyone would sign up for the concerts of groups they liked and if there were too many wanting to attend, the concert crews were determined by seniority.

The Medical Director or a volunteer TERROS doctor would work the concerts with us. After the first concert, he decided that more staff needed training in administering intravenous fluids. Several of the cases we treated at the concert were the result of dehydration, usually the consequence of drugs and heat (remember Phoenix/Tempe summer times are around 113 degrees). The doctor, Sam and I worked out a training program and series of protocols for the use of intravenous medication. About the same time, the doctor decided to add injectable Valium and Antilirium, an antidote to atropine and related drugs, to our list of medications. We also began carrying medications for emergency care of cardiac arrest.

Tom brought a large metal box to contain our medications, syringes, and IV fluids. He had a bolt and chain installed in the ambulance so the drug box could be locked. We didn't want any of our concert going or other clients to help themselves to our supplies. Attending all emergencies now meant carrying Alice the med box with blood pressure equipment, airways, and placebos, an oxygen tank *and* the locked drug box. The staff cartoon depicted Crisis staff with barbells and free weights.

The summer concerts presented an additional challenge for a small agency like ours. We had the crew at the house using the green van, Unit two, providing coverage for the county and several crews at the concert with the ambulance. People at the concert received emergency care and assessment in the aid station. They were then released, transported to the nearest hospital, or transported to the Phoenix house.

It was always disconcerting when a patient had the bad timing to require transport prior to seeing the star attraction of the concert. One man attended every concert—well, sort of attended the concerts. He usually overdosed and required transport about thirty minutes before the main group came on stage. He paid a high price for concert tickets and only saw the warm-up groups! The concert crews would then argue about who was going to transport him to the hospital. Transport meant that we would miss the first part of the concert. Some of these arguments became so fierce that the shouting could be heard above the music. As I've said, we always found something to argue about!

A blue haze usually hung over the concert crowd from the marijuana smoke. Routine outdoor breathing frequently resulted in a contact high, requiring us to sometimes shut ourselves in the aid station listening to the concert through the speakers to avoid becoming loaded. We would take turns regularly circulating through the crowd, watching for signs of overdose. We would return to the aid station after each circuit to breathe non-smoke air and clear our lungs and brains.

Although there was a lot of drug use at the concerts, outbreaks of violence were are. Users tended to stay in groups with similar drug preferences. Junkies hung out with other junkies, speed freaks stayed with speed freaks and tolerated downer freaks. Those who were "tripping" did not really recognize any group. No one would associate with people on PCP or angel dust, except others on PCP. In fact, even most other PCP users avoided other PCP users. Part of the reason for staying in these groups was to be able to acquire, share, and compare their drugs. Some of the more brazen concert attendees/entrepreneurs would wander through the crowd with signs advertising either the desire to sell or buy specific drugs.

One concert evening, Tom radioed in to the Phoenix house that they were transporting a woman to the house for monitoring. About fifteen minutes later, he radioed that the transport was delayed. The woman had stripped off all her clothes and was clinging tightly to a shower pole, singing. They said that they would resume transport as soon as they could pry her loose. We radioed several suggestions for prying a person from a shower pole. Thankfully none of our suggestions resulted in the FCC revoking our license.

The most interesting concert we worked at was in 1976, when we provided the medical backup during some of the filming for the Barbara Streisand version of *A Star is Born* at Arizona State University's Sun Devil stadium. We noticed that the movie crew was shooting a scene in front of where our ambulance was parked in the background and wondered of it would appear in the film. When the movie was released all of the off-duty staff of TERROS attended a screening en masse to find out that we could see our ambulance in the background of one of the scenes. No one in the theatre could understand what we cheered about in that scene. Our staff cartoonist showed the ambulance wearing shades and signing ambulographs for a mob of screaming VWs, mopeds, and Honda Civics.

The following week, Tim and I were dispatched to an unknown overdose. We arrived at the scene and found a small group of people, but no evidence of drugs or alcohol. One of the young women had been talking to her friends when, in mid-conversation, she quit breathing. Within a few seconds, she began breathing and completed the conversation, unaware of the time gap. Everyone denied the use of any substance except cola and 7-UP. Our exam failed to detect the presence of any substance. We were attempting to convince her to go to the hospital when she turned blue again. Tim and I were preparing to perform mouth to mouth and transport when she regained consciousness and began to protest. A person cannot be transported against their will unless they are unconscious or not mentally capable of making the appropriate decision. Tim practically begged her to agree to transport and we finally were granted permission. When we arrived at the hospital, we explained the situation to the triage nurse.

The ER was busy with the one a.m. "BARS ARE CLOSED CROWD." Our client needed to be watched to prevent her from failing to breathe, so we sat in the exam room until the doctor arrived. The doctor looked in the room, shouted, "It's psychosomatic" and walked out. I started chasing the doctor down the hall. Tim called our Medical Director at home and explained the situation, hoping that I would not physically attack the doctor before he completed the call.

We transported our client back to TERROS and explained the situation to Jared. Our doc would come in an hour to examine her. Jared had her sit in the beanless beanbag chair. He sat in front of her with an airway and ambo bag in his hand, staring at her, almost daring her to quit breathing again, until the doctor arrived. She was examined by our doc and a neurologist and the source of the problem was never identified. When we left her at the house, Tim and I went to eat at the all-night restaurant that featured the "Flying Car" a few months earlier. We were people watching as we finished eating when, once again, a car flew through the window. This time the ambulance was spared and the landing strip was unoccupied. The intoxicated driver crawled out of his car and requested a hamburger to go! It was almost two years before I ate at that restaurant at night again.

After we took care of the drunk and filled in the police reports we hopped in the ambulance and radioed that we were en route back to the Phoenix house. Tim and I were still on shift even   though it was almost five a.m. We were dispatched to pick up a man trying to masturbate with a telephone pole. Upon our arrival; I recognized him as the "ghosts in Boise TV" client. As we were transporting him back to County psych, he got up jumped out of the moving ambulance. Tim brought the van to a screeching halt as I bailed out after the client. The man was crawling around on the ground screaming, "MY EYE, MY EYE!" As I was trying to talk him into reentering the van, he picked up what appeared to be a marble. That marble was his missing glass eye. All that time I thought he was hallucinating! Boy, did I feel stupid. It was nine a.m. before we finally got back to officially end our shift.

I was on phone duty one evening when a woman called and said her husband had suddenly "gone crazy." I explained that people suddenly don't go crazy and asked for background information. She said they had gone to Mexico for their twenty-fifth anniversary.

When they returned, her husband had severe diarrhea. The doctor prescribed a drug called Lomotil®. Lomotil is a combination opiate and belladonna agent that can slow the diarrhea. This client did what many of our clients do and that is adopt the attitude "if one pill works, two work better and three will even be best." This client took almost half a bottle because his "butt hurt"!

The client was excitedly describing a thousand people marching in the street with trees growing out of their heads. He said the band was playing some Lawrence Welk songs on high speed. I called Poison Control and checked on the effects of Lomotil. They said I should expect effects similar to opiate overdose. Well, that was certainly not the case. We were seeing the effects of the Belladonna. He was hallucinating and not aware of where he was. I dispatched the ambulance to pick him up and transport him back to the house for treatment. We watched him for about eight hours and then took him and his wife back home with no further problems. We did suggest that he follow the doctor's orders more closely in the future. One thing that a lot of people don't seem to understand is that "the more, the better adage does not apply for medications. Also, just because it is a prescription or even an over-the counter medication doesn't guarantee it is safer.

One time when one of our schizophrenic clients was visiting the house. He started screaming about the CIA monitoring him through TVs. We tried to explain that the TV was off and therefore, the CIA could not trace him. This did not calm him, and in fact, it seemed to enhance the delusions. It became difficult to hear the phones or listen for engines idling in front of the house. Finally, in desperation, we suggested that placing foil on his head would protect him from the CIA. He stood there for about ten minutes quietly, and then his face lit up. He stormed out of the house and slammed the door. He returned about a half hour later with a foil wrapper from Jack in the Box® on his head. The hamburger grease was still dripping from the foil and covered his head and part of his shirt. He had come to thank us for saving him from the demons in the CIA.

Karen returned from her maternity leave and our first shift together after was almost a replica of our last shift together. We were called to an overdose in Glendale, west of Phoenix. En route we had run into a traffic jam and were travelling code three westbound in the eastbound lane. Some driver either didn't see us or was trying to play chicken with us. I drove across the center divider and blew the back tire. I pulled the ambulance to the side of the road and notified base. As we got out of the ambulance, a van pulled up alongside of us and the driver offered us a ride. We grabbed Alice, the drug box, and the oxygen and got into the back of the VW van.

The driver had converted his auto burglar alarm so that it could be triggered from the inside. He explained that he and his wife often slept in their van and wanted to be able to scare off intruders. We sat in the back of the van and he proceeded through traffic with his burglar alarm beeping away. His wife was calmly changing the diapers of their infant on the floor of the van. We bounced along to the scene and discovered it was a game (phony) call. The young man and his wife waited for us to make our determination of the situation drove us back to the ambulance and helped us change the tire. To thank them, we bought them lunch at the restaurant with the flying cars. Luckily, it was early in the day no drunks attempted to turn the restaurant into a drive-thru. Some days were better than others.

GROWING UP

The Crisis clinic was now stocked with a heart monitor and red phone. The red phone was a direct line to the central dispatch for all ambulances, fire departments, and the police. We felt a certain security in that phone because merely knocking it off the hook was a sufficient method to get help. There had been a few occasions when a staff member was home alone and a violent individual had come in. We no longer had to dial for our lives. The dispatcher would send us help immediately. We were also on the rotating ambulance list for emergencies and could be notified by the central dispatcher when we were needed.

Approximately one month after we got the red phone and were placed on the emergency rotation with the other ambulance companies, we were dispatched to JC Penney in the mall. A woman was shopping with her friend and their children. She went into labor, although the baby was early. We walked into the section of the store where they had a display of TVs. There were about five young kids enjoying the multiple TV screens. The manager said the patient was in his office in the back. We walked back and the patient was lying on the floor obviously in labor. We were not able to transport to the hospital because the baby was crowning (the head was showing). We set up and prepared to deliver the baby. After about forty-five minutes a baby girl joined the shopping party. The patient's friend was frantically trying to reach the new father. I walked out and looked at the children sitting in front of the TVs.

"Whose mommy is that back there?" I asked. One of the boys and one of the girls raised their hands. "You have a new baby sister!" I smiled and said to the kids.

The little boy's face fell.

I looked back toward the manager's office and shouted, "Jared, send it back. They don't want it!"

The little boy became so excited that he almost fell off the seat, then suddenly his face changed and he looked frightened. "I think my daddy will be upset!" he said.

That winter, Mitch and Linda were married and Mitch began working part time at a local hospital. Sam and Karen bought one of the original Hondas, the kind only one person could exhale in at a time. Karen went on maternity leave. Air conditioning was finally installed in the house, no more working in a hundred and twenty degree heat; however, it was winter so we didn't really need it yet. I had been promoted to Head staff which, at that time, was a somewhat meaningless position unless something went wrong during a shift.

TERROS adopted uniforms consisting of Levis, shirt, and some type of closed shoe. We were no longer allowed to wear shorts and sandals or the occasional bathing suit to scenes or the hospital. The other ambulance companies began adopting uniforms resembling the police, including little badges. If we had fancy blue uniforms with the badges, our primary clientele would have been returned to the trash can to die.

In South Phoenix a series of gang wars began and responding ambulances were being shot at. I guess the word AMBULANCE on the vehicles did not compensate for the uniforms and badges. Our vehicle was the only one not aerated by bullet holes. The frequent dinner topic when the different crews met was how many bullet holes were in each vehicle. We would smugly reply, "None."

During this time, Jason and I responded to a call from another ambulance company. Their crew had arrived at the scene of an overdose but the uniforms seemed to upset someone in the house. The result was gunfire. As we arrived I felt like I was on the front line of a war. The crew was uninjured but hiding under their ambulance. The police were firing at a house and someone in the house was firing back. We drove alongside the other ambulance as a shield for the crew. They promptly jumped into their unit and drove off. We ignored the police warnings of danger and casually got out of our ambulance and walked toward the house. Somehow the word TERROS on the side of the van provided a safety shield. No one fired in our direction and Jason, the ambulance, and I were untouched. It seemed like a dream, walking through the hail of bullets. Maybe we were just too stupid to be scared.

Inside the house, we worked on the overdosed client while the shooting continued from a different room. It was somewhat unnerving but we resuscitated our client and again walked through the firing line to the ambulance and drove away. The man firing finally surrendered to the police. It is a strange feeling to walk through a situation like that and not feel threatened. My mom was very upset when she saw the TV news that night showing us strolling through the gunfire. She called me at work and screamed so loud that people in the next town could hear her.

As we became more and more sophisticated, with uniforms and a fancy ambulance, we decided to improve our Crisis clinic. Many people seem to insist on an instant cure for their problems. I suppose this makes sense. Once a problem is identified, it should be instantly fixed. No one liked our standard response: "It took you a long time to get this screwed up; it will take a long time to unscrew you."

We installed a glass container on the wall. Inside the container was a magic wand made of cardboard and painted purple with yellow and pink polka dots. We placed a sign above it that read: Break Glass for Instant Cure. We tried to convince one of the crisis staff, a man about six foot six and weighing about three hundred and fifty pounds, to wear a tutu with pink tights and dance out whenever the instant cure was desired. He declined our offer and was very indignant that we had asked. Sometime during that year we acquired a hospital bed, the kind that can be cranked into different positions. We placed the bed and IV pole in the bedroom nearest the crisis clinic. Tori made the mistake of falling asleep in that bed. She awoke when we had cranked the feet and head of the bed to make a perfect V.

Tom announced that we were going to be evaluated by the Joint Commission on Accreditation of Hospitals (JCAH). We would be the first and only non-hospital to be evaluated. He became so nervous that he continually changed policies. He ordered the TV to be placed in the staff lounge, but wanted the staff to sit in the living room in case a body was dumped. I decided that his policy about the TV was ridiculous. That evening, Jason and I carried the TV back to the living room for the benefit of staff, volunteers, and any clients. Tom was very angry the next morning and screamed about my undermining him. Suddenly I found myself en route to New Mexico to conduct a training session. JCAH arrived while I was gone. The inspectors checked our records. They took a break and sat in the staff lounge to watch TV. Their major suggestion was that the TV should be in the living room for the benefit of everyone. We were now accredited and had our TV back! I was even allowed to return from New Mexico.

Chapter 6

Walkin' Walls

Psychedelics and Other Mind Expansion

The shift began with a request to meet the police dispatcher at the station. Upon our arrival, the dispatcher told us that officers participating in a drug bust a few hours earlier that morning had begun "acting weird." We asked for a definition of "acting weird."

"Well, some of the officers are making strange and bizarre radio transmissions. One officer was whistling into the radio, another imitated a cat and dogfight."

Someone at the station decided that the officers had somehow been poisoned during the unsuccessful bust. The sergeant had ordered the officers to return to the station and was successful in getting the officers back with their vehicles intact and no property or personal damage. Poison control had been contacted and referred the call to us. We were requested to check it out. Although the suspect of the drug bust was reported to have been a major drug supplier, he was found to be in possession of nothing except hundreds of pieces of cellophane tape. The officers examined the tape, felt it for some type of hidden substance, and eventually freed the suspected drug dealer.

The cellophane tape actually contained a liquid form of LSD (acid), called windowpane acid. Windowpane can also be found on children's tattoos, stamps, or other types of material that contact the skin. In this case, the LSD was on the cellophane tape. LSD is easily absorbed through skin contact and therefore created a problem for the officers as they examined the tape on the suspected drug dealer. Another form of LSD is "blotter acid," paper impregnated with acid. The paper can be placed on the tongue.

Once it was determined what had happened and that the officers were not in any real trouble, the sergeant called the officers' wives and asked them to pick up their husbands. We provided instructions on the care and feeding of an acid trip to prevent anyone from bumming out. The sergeant called in off-duty replacements and I suspect there was an all-out search for the dealer. We did receive an occasional phone call that day from a wife checking on the treatment plan or asking for reassurance.

We recorded our version of the arrest report in our com log:

STARDATE 26, 2077. SUSPECT ARRESTED CARRYING LARGE QUANTITIES OF CELLOPHANE TAPE. SUSPECT ASSUMED THE POSITION AND OFFICERS PATTING HIM DOWN STUCK TO THE SUSPECT. THROUGH THE EFFORTS OF MANY PERSONNEL, THE STUCKEES WERE REMOVED FROM THE SUSPECT. THE TAPE WAS PEELED OFF AND EXAMINED, RESULTING IN THE SUSPECT CRUMBLING INTO SMALL PIECES OF CARDBOARD. ANOTHER CASE OF HUMPTY–DUMPTITIS!

The house that day was full of off-duty staff watching TV and arguing. It was one of those days in which everyone felt like complaining. Before the program ended, we were called to a very wealthy section of town. Larry pouted because no one would go with him unless he was willing to ride shotgun. I went to the call with one of the off-duty staff. Upon arrival, the husband met us outside and told us that he had returned home from work to find his wife crying uncontrollably, while waving two frying pans in the air.

My partner stayed outside to counsel the husband. I went inside to talk to the wife. I found her in the kitchen with one very large frying pan and one small, doll-sized frying pan. She was wildly waving the pans around, as though she was chasing demons. She kept repeating, "I need to make dinner for my husband." Her frustration was from being unable to decide which pan was larger. She admitted that she had taken acid earlier that day, but she felt fine and no longer loaded. Although she felt unloaded she still had another one to two hours left on her trip. I picked out the correct size frying pan and helped her make dinner.

We explained to her husband that the skill of decision making is deleted from the list of things a person is successful at until they are totally down. We left him with instructions for her care during the " re-entry" portion of her trip. She needed to be reminded that she was still experiencing the effects of a drug and those effects will wear off. She needed a time check. "You will be completely normal in exactly one hour and forty-five minutes." In the sixties and seventies the acid was stronger and a trip frequently lasted eight to twelve hours. The LSD in the eighties became weaker because some of the ingredients were no longer available. Newer acid trips are about four hours long. An eight hour trip made it easy to forget that a drug was taken.

Dropping acid without regard to the set and setting frequently led to "bummers." Often bummers could be treated by simply talking to the person and keeping the lights and sounds low to decrease the sensory stimulation. Sometimes we needed to touch the client but only with permission, to remind them of their realness. We frequently administered a placebo of cherry syrup. We would tell them, "This medicine will numb your nerve endings and quiet your head rushes. It will take about five minutes to work. Are you allergic to anything? This is really important for us to know because, well, you know it is a medicine. Ok. Drink it down quickly and give it five minutes before you feel changes."

We then continued talking and touching and providing just general reassurance, in a mellow environment. Within four minutes, the bummer would describe how their head rushes were mellowed. There are rarely any long term effects after using psychedelic drugs.

Sometimes we were forced to resort to injecting Valium, or using restraints, and brute strength. One young lady dropped acid in a loud, crowded nightclub. When she came onto the acid and was no longer able to determine where she ended and others began, she became panicked and beat up four bouncers. We arrived and radioed that she was very agitated and was being restrained by the very large bouncers! No amount of talking was going to help her, partially because she was yelling so loudly that she couldn't hear us.

We decided that we needed to administer Valium and transport. We injected the Valium and placed her on the gurney. Before the Valium took effect, she almost dismantled our ambulance. Her violent reaction required us to place her face down on the gurney in full restraints. We carefully transported her back to TERROS. She tried to bite us if any of our body parts came too close to her mouth. Two of the bouncers required stitches, but their egos prevented them from admitting that they needed medical attention due to a dinky girl.

Approximately three weeks later we were dispatched to a home where there were four good buddies who had made elaborate plans for an acid trip. They had food for a big feast and were in comfortable surroundings. While waiting to come on to their acid, they began discussing their mutual hobby, skydiving. A big jump was planned for the day after the trip. One of the men began to hypothesize what it would be like to fall and have the chute fail to open. As the men contributed their thoughts on free falling if a chute did not open successfully, one man began to come onto the acid. He envisioned jumping from twenty thousand feet and hitting the earth. He started to live the experience. He decided that you wouldn't just splat, but you'd "splat, bounce, splat." When we arrived at the house, he was bouncing and "splatting" his body on the ground. His head was bouncing on the walls and floor. His friends were able to prevent the onset of their own trip and were attempting to hold him down. Unfortunately he was very strong and as we entered, one of the men was flying through the door.

The helper friend sat on the bummer's legs, he kicked, and the friend flew through the air with the greatest of ease. A new rodeo event! It required a lot of Valium and restraints to transport him. Once he was calm, we were able to assess and treat his other injuries. We were concerned about possible head injuries from his "splatting" his head on the floor.

ABOUT THE DRUGS

Psychedelic drugs like acid (LSD), psilocybin, magic mushrooms ('shrooms), STP, MDA and peyote interact with the brain chemicals that regulate sensory perception. The majority of these drugs are derived from plants.

There is a new group called BATHSALTS which are synthetic drugs related to a stimulant in the khat plant. This plant is from Africa. The people chew the leaves for a mild stimulant effect but the synthetic is much stronger and potentially dangerous. It is sometimes labelled as "jewelry cleaner" or "phone screen cleaner."

Psychedelic users have difficulty distinguishing fact and fantasy. Their sense of direction, distance, and time are distorted. People "tripping" may sound as though they are hallucinating; however, they just perceive life differently. They may have abnormal sensitivity to sensory input and be anxious and panicky. There is rarely any physical reaction, such as convulsions or respiratory depression and no known withdrawals from using psychedelics.

Peyote cactus and mescaline tend to produce delusions involving seeing "god." Some Indian tribes use the buttons from the cactus to prepare for tribal religious ceremonies. Psilocybin and psilocin mushrooms produce similar effects to mescaline. The problems with trying to get high on mushrooms are either the user gets the poisonous Death Cap mushroom or, more often, grocery store mushrooms sprayed with LSD and/or PCP.

DOM, MDA, STP, and MMDA are related to amphetamines and hallucinogens. They produce some of the effects of amphetamines with the addition of intensified sensory changes. Some of these are chemically related to both mescaline (the active ingredient of the peyote cactus) and amphetamines. We would occasionally have clients tripping on one of these drugs. STP stood for serenity, tranquility, and peace; however, none of these occurred while tripping. One of our clients was tripping on STP tried to out run a train. He lost the race.

Looking at patterned wallpaper caused one client to describe "breathing walls." Eating a common chocolate bar may create the same type of drooling, ooh-ing and ahh-ing taste sensations as eating the most expensive white chocolate truffle. Touching smooth tabletops under the influence of acid can be equivalent to running your hand across an unfinished board.

Sensory input is frequently crossed. People may "see" sounds and "hear" visuals. I was once provided a very detailed description of what the color blue sounded like, or what the sound of running water looked like. Disney's movie *Fantasia* reminds me of the type of sensory changes occurring on acid.

Normally, it is easy to determine the boundaries of people and objects in a room. Tripping on psychedelics eliminates this ability. All other persons and objects in a room may have the same single dimension of a sketch or painting. Two or more individuals may appear as some giant person with multiple heads and limbs. Tripping on psychedelics, especially acid makes it difficult to determine where the user ends and others begin. Touching someone on acid without their prior knowledge could result in their panic about growing a third arm.

The brain has a normal filtering mechanism to reduce the amount of stimulation entering at any one time. People do not hear every sound or see every sight. When loaded on psychedelic drugs however, this normal filter is removed and the brain receives all information. Things become very confused! Sometimes it becomes almost impossible to interpret all the input.

Another problem is the inability to pull information from the back of the brain to the forefront. Common life experiences and knowledge are trapped in the deep recesses of the brain. The bladder could be frantically trying to notify the brain that it is time to locate the bathroom, however, the brain will be unable to determine the source and the message being sent. The brain may notify the eye to blink out dust instead of assisting the poor full bladder. The tripper will begin to pace and mumble, "I forgot something, I know I forgot something, (Pace, pace, blink, blink, scratch and think.) I'm just can't remember what I forgot, but I know that I forgot it. I'm just sure that I forgot something."

Tripping on a psychedelic allows the person a chance to be a little crazy for a short period of time. Some trippers may spend their trip speaking in numbers, nursery rhymes, or the alphabet.

"Four, two, nine?"

"No! Little lamb to school."

"Oh, A C G RR."

People may choose to swing on a child's swing set in a three a.m. rainstorm or throw hailstones back at the sky. Psychedelics can remove the seriousness from adulthood. Too bad people don't allow themselves freedom from rigidity more often, unless of course they are loaded.

From the errors of the sixties, acid freaks developed preventative measures to avoid trouble with acid. Preparing for an acid trip requires the appropriate set, setting, and the use of a guide. They arrange for the place to be comfortable, familiar, relaxing, and as non-threatening as possible (the set). They make sure their mental and emotional state is calm, and never drop when worried, tense, scared, or depressed (the setting). They have a good trusted friend (guide) for entertainment and to prevent any possible injury.

One tripper was staring into the fireplace. Her guide wanted to maintain control over the trip and questioned her about her thoughts.

"Based on the laws of physics and philosophy, pushing out the center blue part of the flame will result in the fire becoming cooler."

The tripper then reached for the flame. The guide was able to prevent the heat experiment and probably some major injuries by pointing to the window and yelling, "Look at that bird!" People tripping on acid are more easily distracted than a curious two year old. Now we'll never know if the blue portion of the flame is actually responsible for the heat.

As of this writing, MMDA (Ecstasy) is being evaluated as a valuable tool for the treatment of PTSD (post-traumatic stress disorder). MMDA is a psychedelic with an amphetamine base. It is related to MDA and MDMA. It facilitates communication and reduces fear responses to allow for effective psychotherapy. Psychedelics allow people to deal with their psyche and help the person develop a new perspective on their self and their memories. There are several studies using psychedelics in the treatment of anxiety in patients with terminal illnesses or in patients with autism. They are also being investigated for the treatment of mental illness and depression.

GROWING UP

Our Crisis staff had increased in numbers. Crisis shifts were now only thirty-six hours with a twelve hour on-call and mandatory attendance at staff meetings. Jason had been hired to replace Jared.

I was going to miss Jared's crazy views and com log reports. I worked twenty-four hours per week with Jason and at least once each week, he or I would sustain either major or minor injuries. I think we established a tradition! Jason and I began eating at a local truck stop. I still had my phobia about flying cars. The waitress would watch us and listen for our radio. If we received a call just as our order was ready, she would dump our food into a "to-go" container and throw it at us as we ran out. She would have made an excellent quarterback.

One busy evening, we finally were able to go eat about two-thirty a.m. There were about fifteen truckers in the restaurant when the Hell's Angels arrived. The truckers began commenting on the bikes and long hairs before the Angels entered the diner. As the "Redneck" truckers and "Longhair" bikers slung insults, Jason and I prepared to leave. We crawled under the tables and along the wall as the insults turned to fighting. Once safely inside our ambulance, we radioed for the police and watched from a safe distance. A trucker walked out, got into his truck, and ran over a couple of motorcycles. We drove out behind him, trying to be as inconspicuous as one can be in an ambulance.

We were beginning to conduct regular drug "raps" at area schools for students and at training sessions for the teachers. Once pregnancy testing no longer required blood, we began doing pregnancy tests in crisis. Among the first people we tested were Linda and Karen and they were both positive. It looked like another epidemic was beginning because three detox staff were also pregnant. The rest of the female staff developed paranoia about doorknobs and toilet seats being the cause of pregnancy.

We had been following all of the newspaper accounts of the parent versus school battle over sex education. From our view, there was definitely a lack of and a need for educating preteens. Once it was known that we did pregnancy testing, we saw women from the age of twelve to adult. I found it hard to tell a young kid that she was pregnant. Usually, the kid would respond with, "I couldn't possibly be because ..." and the blank was filled in with some myth; jumping up and down after; douching with coke; eating aspirin before and after; making the male withdraw before ejaculation.

As Linda's pregnancy progressed, Linda and Mitch decided to have a home birth. A very complex system was designed so that Mitch, Tori, Sam, and/or myself could be present to assist. We had to consider all options to ensure that the shift and Linda would be covered. There was the regular on-call and then the "Linda on-call." We used the complex "Linda on-call" twice, but it was false labor.

In the end she had to have a C-section at the hospital.

Chapter 7

LIFE IN THE OZONE

True Hallucinogens

Well it was another exciting summer day. Fifty-seven games of Gin, watching cartoons, and strange phone calls occupied the majority of the morning after we had completed the equipment check. Hot Lips was in a foul mood, slamming things around and not talking to anyone. Some prepubescent individual called seventeen times asking about underwear.

"What color underwear are you wearing?"

Our response ranged from "None" to "Lime green with baby shit yellow stripes."

In the Detox area, two clients were arguing about who had a bigger habit. There were a few calls complaining about a new street drug that didn't produce the high expected from the sales pitch. We identified the pill as Ortho-Novum birth control pills. After we hung up the phone, we discussed all the things we really wanted to say about trying to get high on birth control pills.

During this absolutely thrilling period of time, two men entered the house. One of the men, Fred, walked as though he was carrying a thousand raw eggs between his legs and under his arm pits. Fred's friend seemed to be working very hard at not laughing hysterically. There were two other men outside laughing and carrying on. I had the feeling that the day was about to become interesting.

As we were examining Fred, his friend told us how Fred managed to receive his unique injuries. The four men had been planning to take a camping trip for several weeks. A few hours prior to the departure, Fred had eaten Jimson weed, also known as Loco weed (belladonna or atropine). The men were aware that Fred ate the Jimson weed, but they went camping anyway. None of the men were sure of the effects, although they heard you could get REALLY HIGH! The men didn't think Fred could get into a lot of trouble in the desert, so they weren't too worried when he took off from the group. After all, the only things to possibly harm Fred were rattlesnakes, cacti, and jackrabbits.

Fred's buddies set up the campsite and prepared the campfire. When the sun sets in the desert, the temperature drops drastically because there is no cover to retain the heat. One of the men remarked that they had not seen Fred in several hours and it was going to get dark relatively soon. They decided to go looking for Fred. They found a trail of Fred's clothes, intensifying their concern. One of the rules of desert survival is to keep your clothes on to avoid overheating. Fred was wandering without clothes and without water. Violation of desert survival rules of water and clothing can certainly shorten one's lifespan. It took approximately an hour and half to find Fred.

Upon locating Fred, their alarm changed to incredulous stares and finally to hysteria! Fred was fondling a Saguaro Cactus and whispering sweet nothings into the thorns. He was having sex with the cactus. Saguaro cacti are a protected species, although I am not sure that fondling the cactus can be considered an act that will endanger the plant. Fred told his friends that it was a "free all you can do night." He believed that he was in a brothel and the Saguaro Cacti were the women working there. Apparently those sharp women were quite alluring, although I don't think the cacti appreciated his sexual appetite! No one knows how many "women" Fred was charmed by or . . . could this be high fiber sex? Fred's friends did not immediately remove Fred from his current sexual, uh, partner. They said they were busy commenting on his positions and technique and laughing.

Eventually, his friends carefully dragged him back to camp, attempting to avoid the social diseases one gets from sexual contact with cacti. All the way back to camp, Fred described the women and his activities. His friends found all of his clothing, some of it worn by several Prickly Pear Cacti. After dressing Fred, they put him in a sleeping bag and zipped it up, hoping to keep him safe. They rolled a joint and laughed about Fred's adventures. No one could imagine the pain he would experience upon his return to earth.

Fred rolled over into the campfire and began "rafting down the Colorado River." As he rowed his boat around the rocks in the water, his friends jumped into action to save him when the sleeping bag caught fire. Although it can seem difficult unzipping a sleeping bag during the night when the bathroom calls, it is virtually impossible to rapidly remove someone from a burning sleeping bag, during a non-water rafting trip. By the time he was brought to us, Fred's trip had almost completely ended. He was becoming more lucid and starting to experience the pain of thousands of cactus thorns in his chest and private parts, the intense sunburn pain, and the burns from the campfire.

Fred had no idea of how he obtained his injuries and he did not believe what his friend was relating. However, he could not offer another explanation for either the thorns or the burns. The entire story was related to us punctuated by laughter and snickering. Fred, on the other hand, alternated grimaces and outbursts of pain with, "I'd never do that!" We mentally divided Fred in half, difficult to do when stifling laughter, and spent three very long hours pulling out thorns and treating burns. Our empathy was overwhelmed by images of the adventures with cacti.

STARDATE 27, 5265. THE PLANET CACTUVIOUS HAS SOME VERY PRICKLY FLIRTATIONS AND NEW SEXUAL POSITIONS.

One evening Steve and I responded to a tricyclic antidepressant overdose. Steve and I were unable to convince this woman to go to the hospital so we decided to wait until she began hallucinating, thus giving us implied consent for transport. The law would not allow us to transport someone against their will unless they are unconscious or not lucid.

We told her what our plans were but she still refused our aid, yet she still did not throw us out. Once she began to hallucinate we loaded her onto the litter and started down the four flights of fancy circular stairs. A gurney weighs about fifty pounds without a patient. Since gurneys are not easily carried down a narrow circular staircase we would use a litter, the narrow type used by the military. Steve was taller than I, and in order to carry the litter level I had to hold it above my ears. Before we reached the third floor, she began to have seizures.

Litters are very narrow and not designed for the patient to be able to move around. As I navigated down a circular staircase, carrying a litter and this two-hundred-pound woman was violently flopping above my ears. Steve was twisting and turning the litter, trying to keep her from flipping off, as if she were a small goldfish he was trying to slide into water. We finally reached the ground floor, started an IV and began administering medications at the foot of the steps. The crowd scene almost prevented us from making it to the ambulance before she coded. The drugs we administered kept her alive until we arrived at the hospital. Although we managed to save her that time, she successfully committed suicide about one month later. I really think that I saw more   people die from tricyclic overdoses than from any street drug.

There are "a million stories in the naked city" and hallucinogen stories are the most fun ones to relate. Larry and I returned to the house one day and found Tori with three clients. The clients were making strange motions in the center of the living room. Tori explained that they had all eaten Jimson weed and they were washing a VW. We watched them finish the wash job and beg to wax this non-existent vehicle. Suddenly, one of the clients tried to climb up the inside of the fireplace. He blathered about going into his apartment. Larry was attempting to get him out of the fireplace when one of the others screamed, "DUCK! Here they come!" and fell on the floor.

In my best imitation of a war movie, I ducked too and tried to become a part of the underside of the couch. Oh well, I guess it was good to know that my reflexes were still intact. Larry responded by jumping and hitting his head on the fireplace. Tori was laughing so hard that she was no help to either of us. There I was, five hours into a twenty-four hour shift and ready to be committed to a psych ward! Several staff members began wandering in to visit. They were confused about why I was trying to crawl under the couch, Larry was complaining about the fireplace, and Tori was laughing hysterically. The clients were now lined up by the desk, waiting for a trolley. The clients complained bitterly about the trolley service in Phoenix. Once I crawled out from under the couch, I joined them in their complaints. Boy, do I love to complain!

The visiting staff assisted us with the atropine bummers and when the drug effects wore off, the clients were sent home. We all settled down to watch TV. Maybe it would be a good night after all.

One of our busiest shifts was affectionately known as the "Field Trip." A class from a private school took a field trip to the Botanical Gardens. Several students recognized Jimson weed and took a side trip. They introduced Jimson weed to their other classmates and eventually there were a dozen students visiting another galaxy. Each atropine bummer is equivalent to forty-two hyperkinetic two-year-old children eating seventy-five candy bars. They are very active and need to be watched constantly. We had TWELVE ATROPINE BUMMERS IN THE HOUSE AT THE SAME TIME AND THREE STAFF! We called in all of the off-duty personnel foolish enough to answer their phone and quickly trained the teachers in care and management of people tripping on the atropine.

There were people walking into the walls yelling, "Let me in, damnit." There were students standing by the door of the bathroom screaming, "Turn green!" A few kids were sliding down the rickety banister and others were "constructing" something. They even "hit their thumb with the hammer" and swore while shaking their hand. Someone found the paint we were using to paint the living room and was running through the house screaming, "Oh my God, he melted Jeffrey!" Damn, they moved fast. Someone lifted a chair and was searching for the steering wheel. Others were ducking flying saucers or bats or some other unknown projectiles. I must have survived that shift because I am typing this, but I'm not positive how.

The students were tripping for almost twenty-four hours and no one slept during that entire time. Fortunately, we had no other calls that night. Maybe there was a god looking out for us. I think that Botanical Gardens were no longer on the list of approved field trips for any child over seven. Either that or they removed the Jimson weed. Unfortunately, Jimson weed grows wild. There is a green pod in the center of the plant and the pod contains seeds that are composed of atropine, scopolamine, and hycosamine.

STARDATE 31, 2133. House attacked by killer tomatoes!

Jason and I worked a twenty-four hour shift the day Nixon made his famous resignation speech. It was definitely no ordinary shift, although now that I think about it, ordinary is difficult to define. As I walked into the house, I heard Jason in the back of the house yelling, "You can't walk around like that!" I knew I should have left, when Jason and his client appeared, the client was walking around holding his penis. His penis had been tattooed like a barber pole, red and white stripes, and the client was waving it in circles as if he were directing a plane to land. Tripping on atropine certainly makes people do strange things.

While Jason was chasing the barber pole, I answered the phone. The person on the other end of the line was asking about a drug he had just bought on the street. He wanted to know if he could get high on Pitocin®, a drug used only in hospitals to stimulate labor. I was trying very hard not to laugh, but it was difficult. The only thing I could say was, "If you're pregnant, you will become unpregnant. If you aren't pregnant, you might cramp a lot. If you're male, no one knows what will happen; maybe you will find your penis under the pillow in the morning. Call me tomorrow and let me know what happens."

I alerted the other staff that a hospital pharmacy had been ripped off and to be prepared for some big time drug problems. During my attempt at tact and professionalism, translated trying not to laugh at "getting high on Pitocin®," a man about twenty-eight years old walked in. He was about six-foot-six inches and very muscular. Something seemed to have upset him and he was trying to explain but was not able to communicate well. He picked up the large straight back chair and held it over his head while screaming at me. Unfortunately nothing he said made much sense and I finished my phone conversation. I nicely asked him to put the chair down and when that didn't work I got tough. My voice kept getting louder and he threatened me with the chair.

I heard Jason trying to march his "barber pole" in my direction to check on me, but the "barber pole" was watching the space ship land in the bathroom. Finally, I stood up, brought my shoulders up, and placed my fists on my hips. I growled, "You either put that chair down or I'll stuff it up your left nostril!" For a second, the only sounds were those of the "barber pole" providing landing directions to the spacecraft. The ape looked at the chair and set it down very gently and then sat like a young child hoping to show his halo. He then began explaining his problem, he had stubbed his toe on some loose board at the apartment and his landlord refused to fix the board. Waving a chair and yelling certainly seemed like a perfectly acceptable response to a stubbed toe for him!

The phones continued to ring and Linda, our partner, entered the house after checking the ambulance. She began answering the phones, I talked with "stubbed toe" and Jason chased "barber pole." About an hour before Nixon was scheduled to speak, our clients left. Twenty minutes before the speech, the phone calls ended. Suddenly, there was absolutely nothing, no traffic, no phone calls, no clients. This eerie quiet remained until about three-thirty a.m. Jason and I played one hundred and twenty-one games of gin and Linda typed a term paper.

About ten-thirty p.m., I think we had played forty-five games of gin and Jason was hungry. We went to our favorite Carrow›s restaurant. We met another ambulance crew at Carrow's and they described the same kind of eerie night. Although neither ambulance crew was busy, we still completed our full dinner in less than fifteen minutes. Emergency health personnel share the same dietary habits. Regardless of whether they are on duty or not, emergency workers can eat a full three course dinner in less than fifteen minutes. We are almost finished eating when other people are still buttering their rolls. I think that explains why we were not invited out to eat with normal folks very often. When we were busy, Jason and I could eat a hamburger, fries, salad, and coffee in less than five minutes. The stomach could finish chewing what we swallowed whole.

ABOUT THE DRUGS

Atropine is one of the Belladonna alkaloids or deadly nightshade. Plants in this family include tomatoes, potatoes, and eggplant. In small doses, these chemicals are very useful medically, however, they are poisonous in large doses.

Medicinally these plants are used to treat gastrointestinal disorders, diarrhea, asthma, migraines, nocturnal incontinence, muscle spasms, Parkinson's disease, and motion sickness.

Symptoms of an atropine bummer, or poisoning, include high fever, widely dilated pupils, dry skin from a breakdown of the sweating mechanism, no ability to remember what occurred, hallucinations or as we say, "life in the ozone," and no pain sensations. Most people who abuse these chemicals do so only once. There is no enjoyment in tripping when one loses seventy-two hours and cannot remember what happened or why cast, splints, or other dressings are present on their body. Unfortunately the street drug information only describes what drugs can be used to hallucinate with and how to recognize the plants containing the drugs. There is no mention of the loss of time and probable injury.

Although the drugs create a high fever and elevated blood pressure, we were never able to obtain the actual values. It is estimated that the body temperature can reach as high as 110°. One of the volunteers ignored the training information about atropine bummers and attempted to take a patient's temperature with a glass thermometer (the only kind available). The patient began eating the thermometer and had to be transported to the hospital for the removal of glass and mercury. One patient stuck the thermometer in his ear. In those days, we did not have thermometers that registered the temperature on the forehead. Another patient tried to eat the blood pressure cuff. Often the patient will begin flexing their arm and jumping around when they have a blood pressure cuff on. These behaviors make it very difficult to monitor the vital signs of "atropine bummers."

Among the drugs in this group are the antihistamines commonly found in every drugstore, grocery store, and convenience mart. One young woman ingested an entire bottle of Contac® cold capsules and some alcohol. She literally bounced through the doorway yelling, "Make way for the queen! Make way for a checkmate!" The woman spent seven hours jumping around the living room, generally in a diagonal direction, shouting, "Checkmate!!! Check!!! Checkmate!!" I think we were playing chess, but I never found my knight, pawn, or bishop. I gave up on the queen and king. Maybe we should have recorded her moves for the next International Chess Tournament.

The other group of drugs in this category are tricyclic antidepressants, such as Elavil®. They are not related to Belladonna, but act on similar brain chemicals. They are prescribed for severe depression resulting from a decrease in brain chemicals. Although the overdose symptoms include hallucinations similar to atropine, we saw more dangerous symptoms including cardiac arrhythmias (heart beating out of rhythm) and seizures. Whereas the other hallucinogens are taken once for a good time and are never repeated, these drugs are often abused for intent to commit suicide. Generally if we aided someone overdosed on tricyclics, they were resentful at our interference and frequently repeated the effort at a later time.

Chapter 8

Dusted

Phencyclidine or PCP

Jason and I were playing our usual game of gin and discussing the strange vibes we both felt. Both of us felt that something was going to happen during the shift to threaten our anatomical structure. Although the day had not started off well. Baby Huey attempting to tie our ambulance antennae into a knot, we had absolutely no good reason for this feeling of doom. At about ten p.m., Kate dispatched us to a possible acid bummer. Martha, a new volunteer, carne along for the experience.

As we neared the location, we could hear roaring and screaming, with an occasional crash-bang-thud. Jason radioed that we were on the scene and were going to evaluate. He requested that Kate remain ready to summon help quickly. We took Alice, the med box, and cautiously approached the house. My heart was racing and Jason was sweating. A woman suddenly appeared from the dark, began flailing her arms about and yelled at us to hurry. She wasn't making a great deal of sense, but we knew from her actions, and the background sounds, there was some urgency. The roaring and screaming were coming from inside the house, and the banging, crashing, and strange thuds increased in both frequency and intensity. We were hoping that maybe lions had broken into the house and we could just call Animal Control and let them handle it, but we knew we had to go in anyway. We told Martha to stay behind us until we knew what was happening.

The woman told us that her boyfriend was alone inside the house and was tripped out. During her frenzied explanation, I peered through the slight opening of the drawn curtains in an effort to determine what was happening. It was difficult to believe that all of the sounds were coming from just one person. The interior of the house had been demolished, probably by Godzilla from the looks of it. The curtain rod from the back window was knotted and lying on the floor. The remains of a door were stacked in a corner and the carpeting was shredded. The kitchen sink was in the center of the living room. I was trying to convey the magnitude of the destruction to Jason without frightening the woman further. Suddenly I was peering at a pair of legs. As I began my upward glance, checking out what was attached to the legs, I found myself staring at a six foot plus, highly muscular, naked man!

I was only five foot three, Jason was about five foot four. This was going to be very challenging. A momentary flash of insanity crossed the path of my peripheral vision. It was Martha who was four foot ten and could no longer stay behind. I wondered if there was a stepstool handy so we could make eye contact with Godzilla.

Jason and I conferred and decided that it would be safer if we could get the man out of the house, rather than us attempting to enter. Suddenly we realized that the woman and Martha had disappeared. We both began to swear, but before we could start to search, Martha ran from behind the house. She yelled that the woman had entered through the back door. We ran around to the back, telling the neighbors to return to their homes. Jason opened the door slightly and spotted the woman crouched on the floor in the corner of the kitchen. We could see that the results of Godzilla's rampage were extensive.

The woman appeared frozen in the corner. Godzilla was in the other room, so I crawled in to get the woman. I couldn't get her to move, so I stood to lift her. Before I could reach my full height, Jason yelled, "Duck!!" and I fell to the floor. As I hit the ground, and Amana side-by-side refrigerator freezer flew overhead. Funny how observant we sometimes become. I crawled out, dragging the woman with me. My heart beat could be heard in the next county! Damn, I'm glad I responded and didn't ask, "WHY?"

Jason radioed that we needed assistance, men, lots of men! Big, tall, huge, giant men! Kate dispatched both the police and fire departments. The fire fighters arrived first and stood behind me until the police arrived. Once again, I kept checking my back for the sign that said parade leader. We explained what was happening and the firefighters volunteered to wait for the police.

I think someone was on the corner selling tickets because the crowd had gotten too large to be just a group of neighbors. When the police arrived, one of them noticed the large number of observers and attempted crowd control. He walked through the crowd, shined his flashlight in each person's eyes and said, "Go home." Certainly would have convinced me to leave.

Everyone agreed that the woman should call and attempt to get her friend out of the house. In her frightened attempt at seductiveness, she kept saying, "John, please John." She called his name for at least five minutes. The only other sounds we heard were thuds, roars, and crash-bangs. John soon appeared at the screen door. An officer shined his flashlight toward the man. Concerned about the possibility of weapons, the officer swept his flashlight in an upward motion along the man's frame, until he realized that the man was naked. Suddenly his flashlight was focused on the stars and the cop shouted, "He's got no clothes on!"

I was glad the cop announced it for those folks still lining up for their tickets to the show. The woman continued to call and John finally walked out with his arms out stretched, reminiscent of Lon Chaney in *The Mummy*. The cops surrounded him and he was quickly handcuffed behind his back and led to the ambulance. Someone wrapped a blanket around him as he walked. He was laid facedown on the squad bench in the ambulance.

When we began our transport, I radioed Kate to notify the County Hospital to have security waiting for us. I was not comforted by the line of police following us. The ambulance was a much smaller area to wreck and could have been destroyed before the cops had ever parked their cars. Jason sat next to John, attempting to get any information he could. Jason asked, "When were you born?" The response was, "The moment I knew."

We arrived safely at the hospital and were greeted by the security guards. As we were climbing out of the ambulance, preparing to place John on the hospital gurney, he began scratching his head with one hand, the other hand still behind his back. The broken handcuff was dangling from his wrist. Jason, Martha, and I had an instantaneous look of panic when we realized that he could have demolished us and the ambulance without any effort. The officer who owned the broken handcuff was trying to figure out how his superiors were going to accept the explanation, "Bad guy broke handcuff by scratching his head." I always thought there was some special super metal alloy used to make handcuffs and the purpose of cuffing behind the back was for safety, but that experience certainly shot down that theory.

John was taken to the quiet room by the guards and police. We gave the little information we had to the hospital staff. There seemed to be some shuffling noises, then the police walked out laughing. Our friend had urinated all over the ceiling, like an indignant male child.

That was our first known case of phencyclidine (PCP or Angel Dust) but it certainly wasn't our last.

One afternoon, a young woman on PCP walked into the house and looked very puzzled. She said, "I don't understand it. I'm walking down the street and people point at me and scream or puke. I think I'm dressed." In my most tactful and professional manner, I'm pointing and sounding like someone ready to puke. During EMT and paramedic training, we are constantly reminded not to invoke our x-ray vision and record that some bone was broken. We were to use qualifiers such as "It appears to be broken" to avoid being accused of diagnosing. This woman's femur was split in half and both ends were sticking out of her leg! ("It appeared to be broken.") She was not limping, and did not appear to be in pain. She was very confused by my medical evaluation which consisted of me saying, "UGGGH," and it just didn't seem to be soothing to her. As a tribute to Jared and the Star Trek-ism Com Log, this was recorded as:

STARDATE 5094.6. CROSSBONES ENTERED THE PREMISES. SKULL AND PIRATE SHIP TO BEAM UP LATER.

Because PCP is inexpensive to manufacture, it can be sold as any drug for the going rate of the selected drug. It also can be profitable at $0.50 per hit. People frequently obtained dust instead of their favorite drug and we were placed into some precarious and deadly positions. Phencyclidine does create both homicidal and suicidal behavior and I suspect it is a major contributing factor to our large prison population. Probably the most difficult aspect of phencyclidine is that it requires a spinal tap to reliably determine its presence in an individual. Spinal taps are tricky under the best conditions. Trying to perform a tap when the patient is threatening to throw a five hundred pound gurney is less than ideal.

The effects of PCP vary both within a particular individual and between different individuals. Sometimes people are mute. One man could only moo like a cow for the four hours he was in our agency.

Dust commonly causes people to have death-oriented trips. The user does not talk about death as a terminal patient would, but rather as though he has already died. They will suddenly turn and scream, "How dare you talk to me that way! Have you no respect for the dead?! St. Peter has invited me in and you can't blow it for me now!"

One man was standing in the middle of the street in a catatonic state. The cops carried him to the shoulder of the road and radioed for us. While they awaited our arrival, the client began humping the telephone pole. Before he could be stopped, he attacked the officers and in mid punch resumed his catatonic stance.

We were dispatched to an auto accident early one Sunday morning. The car had been driven under a flatbed truck and essentially had been crushed. We predicted that the individual occupying the squashed vehicle was dead. Peering through the openings once occupied by glass, we noticed some movements of the chest. I reached in and felt for the carotid artery in the man's neck. There was a faint pulse. The firefighters had pried open the car with the Jaws of Life and we began to immobilize the driver. We established an airway and started an IV. We very carefully lifted the man out of the car and set the backboard on the gurney. Jason radioed the results of our examination. Suddenly, the man jumped off of the gurney and began to run down the street!! He fell dead about a half of a block down the road. When we received the results of the autopsy, we were flabbergasted. According to the coroner, the man should have died immediately upon the impact because he severed his brainstem, the part controlling respiration and heartbeat. The toxicology report indicated the presence of phencyclidine.

ABOUT THE DRUGS

Phencyclidine was developed in the late fifties as a human anesthetic. It was removed from the market in 1965. During the clinical trials of phencyclidine, patients would get up during surgery and beat the tar out of the surgeon or they would try and dismantle the recovery room. This created some distress among the surgeons.

Ketamine is a relative of phencyclidine and is used to start and maintain anesthesia by producing a trance-like state. Ketamine is approved for use both in controlled medical or veterinary medicine. There are some clinical trials using ketamine in treating PTSD and status epilepticus seizures.

Although phencyclidine has been around for many years we still do not understand it. It rapidly enters into the spinal fluid bathing the brain and remains there. Dusted people are very unpredictable because the amount of drug in the brain at any given moment varies. PCP can act like speed, downers, or hallucinogens. There is no pain sensation and generally no awareness of one's body.

Chapter 9

Odds and Ends

Epilogue

Mr. Clean resigned from Detox and moved to Alaska. The rumor is he decided to mine for gold. Pat became the new Detox Director. I really liked Pat although he was too pushy sometimes. He had been with the agency as a Detox counselor before I ever started. During his early years with TERROS he seemed to be recuperating from Vietnam. Eventually he joined the closet college kids and enrolled in school. He was finishing his studies in social work when he was selected to become Detox Director. He eventually left TERROS and became a counselor with Vietnam vets.

One beautiful Sunday afternoon, Pat, Tom, and Steve went hiking in South Mountain Park. Steve worked for the State Department of Health and Emergency Services and spent a lot of time visiting with us. Jessie was working his first shift. He had heard all the horror stories about my temperament and was the nervous, new kid on the block working with the TYRANT. He was checking the ambulance supplies, or avoiding me, when Steve called. Tom had fallen down the mountain and appeared to have fractured his leg. Steve was going to meet us at the entrance gate and direct us to the site. Jessie trembled all the way to South Mountain Park, hoping I wouldn't expect him to name all two hundred and six bones in the body. Jessie didn't understand that although I quizzed the people training for their paramedic or EMT II, I was kinder to the new kids.

We arrived at the park with our lights and sirens blaring. We could see Steve's jeep rapidly approaching. Before we could drive into the park, the Park Ranger stopped us. He stood in front of the ambulance and demanded the admission fee! We certainly appeared to be people out for a Sunday picnic. Jessie and I were a week away from payday and had about thirty-seven cents in our combined fortune. Steve was screaming at the Ranger as Jessie and I sat listening to the sirens.

We promised the Ranger that we would not smile or do anything that would be slightly suggestive of enjoying ourselves. The foolish Ranger just stood in front of a blaring ambulance demanding the dollar admission fee. I was tempted to convert the Ranger into a pancake, Steve was screaming insults and threatened to sue. We found twenty cents in the med box and added it to our thirty-seven cents. Steve kicked in his last fifty cents. We followed Steve to the place where Tom fell. I hiked down and checked Tom while Jessie was getting the necessary equipment from the ambulance. Pat began harassing me and became a general nuisance. I finally told him to go boil some water. Pat started down the hill, stopped and thought about it, and returned to make me crazy. My next suggestion was that he find something else to do or I was going to push him down the mountain head first. Jessie decided to protect Pat and assigned him some useless task.

We decided that it was too dangerous to move. Tom because he was in severe shock from the pain and blood loss. We radioed for fire and Life Flight. The fire medics arrived and administered pain medication. This was the one time that I was sorry we refused to carry pain medication. It seemed like it took a month to move Tom from the mountain. When we finally got Tom off of the mountain, I wondered if Life Flight had to pay the admission fee. How did the Ranger stop the fire truck and helicopter? "I'm sorry you can't hover in this area unless you drop the money into my cash register. It'll be an extra dollar for the dust you move."

Tom had a bad reaction to his pain medication and the hospital had to restrain him. He began to hallucinate and was trying to protect himself from the aliens. He managed to drive his traction weights into the wall. We were called to counsel the crazy director of TERROS.

After Tom was discharged and his leg healed, he accepted a job as manager with an airplane manufacturer in California.

Steve completed his M.B.A. He and Hot Lips decided to enter the corporate world. Hot Lips opened her own accounting firm. Jamie Sue, one of the crisis staff members, initially became Director of Crisis. She decided to return to a career in nursing after directing the Crisis Department for two years. Jason was Director of Crisis for a year, then became the Director of an Alcohol Recovery Program.

When I resigned to complete my formal education in California, we had fifteen staff members obtain degrees in nursing, twenty-two staff members receive degrees in social work or counseling, and three staff graduate as Physician Assistants. Although I have completed the requirements for my doctorate in pharmacology-toxicology, I think my greatest education was acquired in the six years I spent at TERROS.

Denise (Deni) Gordon was born and raised in Phoenix, Arizona. She graduated from Arizona State University with Bachelor and Master of Science degrees. While completing her degrees she began working at Terros, first as a volunteer than as paid staff. Terros is a drug abuse agency that provides detox, counseling, free clinic and emergency crisis and medical services. Terros still provides most of the same services, medical care and help for people with substance abuse and mental health issues.

Upon completing her Master's degree, she moved to Northern California to attend a Ph.D. program in Pharmacology/Toxicology at UCDavis. Her EMT license was current and she became the first female firefighter/EMT on the volunteer Fire Department in Dixon, Ca. She still lives in Northern California.

She taught nursing pharmacology at night at Solano College and seventh grade science during the day. She has three K9 children and various indoor and outdoor fish. She loves to downhill ski, travel, and garden. She fell in love with downhill skiing because gravity did all the work and because in Phoenix snow comes in a paper cone with flavors.

www.ingramcontent.com/pod-product-compliance
Lightning Source LLC
Chambersburg PA
CBHW022119280326
41933CB00007B/460

9 781949 290172